The Sixth Book of Moses and The Seventh Book of Moses

By

Johann Scheibel

First published in 1849

Published by Left of Brain Books

Copyright © 2023 Left of Brain Books

ISBN 978-1-397-66528-7

First Edition

All rights reserved. No part of this publication may be reproduced, distributed, or transmitted in any form or by any means, including photocopying, recording, or other electronic or mechanical methods, without the prior written permission of the publisher, except in the case of brief quotations permitted by copyright law. Left of Brain Books is a division of Left Of Brain Onboarding Pty Ltd.

PUBLISHER'S PREFACE

About the Book

"The Sixth and Seventh Books of Moses are two grimoires allegedly dictated to Moses along with the Torah (the first five books of Moses).

Published as volume 6 of "Bibliothek der Zauber-Geheimniss- und Offenbarungs-Bucher, etc." in 1849 in Stuttgart by antiquarian Johann Scheibel, these books contain numerous allegedly magical spells used to summon spirits to do the will of the conjourer. Although these are allegedly Kabbalistic in nature, there is very little or no influence of Kabbala within the pages. The texts are allegedly translated from a text written in the Cuthan-Samaritan language, a language considered extinct since the 12th century. No manuscripts older than 1849 are to be found, and the claimed origin must be regarded pseudepigraphic and spurious.

The included pictures of the "seals" consist of various stylized symbols surrounded pseudo-hebrew and pseudo-latin phrases and letters. The Latin language wasn't spoken in the area of Judea where Moses lived. The pictures of the seals are therefore by necessity of different origin than what is claimed."

(Quote from wikipedia.org)

CONTENTS

PUBLISHER'S PREFACE

THE SIXTH BOOK OF MOSES 1

   INTRODUCTION 2
      THE MYSTERY OF THE FIRST SEAL 5
      THE MYSTERY OF THE SECOND SEAL....................................... 7
      THE MYSTERY OF THE THIRD SEAL 9
      THE MYSTERY OF THE FOURTH SEAL...................................... 11
      THE MYSTERY OF THE FIFTH SEAL 13
      THE MYSTERY OF THE SIXTH SEAL.. 15
      THE MYSTERY OF THE SEVENTH SEAL 17

THE SEVENTH BOOK OF MOSES.. 19

      THE TWELVE TABLES OF THE SPIRITS 20
      EXTRACT FROM THE MAGICAL KABALA 32
      TREATISE SION.. 51
      TREATISE OF THE SIXTH BOOK OF MOSES............................ 55
      TREATISE OF THE SEVENTH BOOK OF MOSES 61
      BIBLIA ARCANA MAGICA ALEXANDER 75
      MAGICAL (SPIRIT COMMADO) BESIDE THE BLACK RAVEN 85
      THE RABELLINI TABLE 99

THE SIXTH BOOK OF MOSES

INTRODUCTION

MOSES' MAGICAL SPIRIT-ART

Translated from the Ancient Hebrew

The Seven Seals of the Spirits

MAGIA ALBA ET NIGRA UNIVERSALIS SEU NECROMANTIA

THAT is, that which embraces the whole of the White and Black Art, (Black Magic,) or the Necromancy of all Ministering Angels and Spirits; how to cite and desire the nine Choruses of the good angels and spirits, Saturn, Jupiter, Mars, Sun, Venus, Mercury, and Moon.

The most serviceable angels are SALATHEEL, MICHAEL, RAPHAEL, URIEL, together with the Necromancy of the black magic of the best Ministering Spirits in the Chymia et Alchymia of Moses and Aaron.

That which was hidden from David, the father of Solomon, by the High Priest SADOCK, as the highest mystery, but which was finally found in the year 330 A.D., among others, by the first Christian Emperor Constantine the Great, and sent to Pope Sylvester at Rome, after its translation under Julius II, Pontifice Maximus. Typis Manabilis sub poena excommunicationis de numquam public imprimendis sent to the Emperor Charles V., and highly recommended in the year 1520 A.D., approved by Julii II, duos libros quos Mosis condidit arter artistis summus sedalitate SADOCK. Libri hi colorum sacra sunt vota sequenter spiritus omnipotens qui uigil illa facit at est sumis pia necessaria. Fides.

Instruction

These two Books were revealed by God, the Almighty, to his faithful servant Moses, on Mount Sinai, intervale lucis, and in this manner they also came into the hands of Aaron, Caleb, Joshua, and finally to David and his son Solomon and their high priest Sadock. Therefore, they are Biblis arcanum arcanorum, which means, Mystery of all Mysteries.

The Conversation of God

Adonai, Sother, Emanuel, Ehic, Tetragramaton, Ayscher, Jehova, Zeboath, the Lord of Hosts, of Heaven and Earth; that which appertains to the Sixth and Seventh Books of Moses, as follows:

Adonai, E El, Zeboath, Jebaouha, Jehovah, E El, Chad, Tetragramaton Chaddai, Channaniah, al Elyon, Chaye, Ayscher, Adoyah Zawah, Tetragramaton, Awiel, Adoyah, Chay, Yechal, Kanus, Emmet. Thus spake the Lord of Hosts to me Moses.

Eheye, Ayscher, Jehel, Yazliah, Ellion. Sum qui sum ab aeterno in aeternum, thou my servant Moses, open thou thine ears, hear the voice of thy God. Through me Jehovah, Aglai, the God of heven and earth, thy race shall be multiplied and shall shine as the stars of heaven. In addition to this I will also give thee might, power and wisdom, to rule over the spirits of heaven and hell.

Over the ministering angels and spirits of the fourth element as well as of the seven planets. Hear also the voice of thy God wherewith I give thee the seven seals and twelve tables. Schem, Schel, Hamforach, that the angels and spirits may always yield obedient service to thee, when thou callest upon them and citest them by these seven seals and twelve tables of my omnioptence; and hereunto thou shalt also have herewith a knowledge of the highest mysteries.

Therefore, thou, my faithful friend, dear Moses, take thou the power and high might of thy God.

Aclon, Ysheye, Channanyah, Yeschayah, E El, Elijon, Rachmiel, Ariel, Eheye, Ayscher, Eheye, Elyon. Through my Seals and Tables.

THE MYSTERY OF THE FIRST SEAL

Seal of the Choir of the Ministering Archangels

CONJURATION

I, N.N., a servant of God, desire, call upon the OCH, and conjure thee through water, fire, air, and earth, and everything that lives and moves therein, and by the most holy names of God, Agios, Tehirios, Perailtus, Alpha et Omega, Beginning and End, God and Man-Sabaoth, Adanai, Agla, Tetragramaton, Emanuel, Abua, Ceus, Elioa, Torna, Deus Salvator, Aramma, Messias, Clerob, Michael, Abreil, Achleof, Gachenas et Peraim, Eei Patris et Peraim Eei filii, et Peraim Dei spiritus Teti, and the words by which Solomon and Manasses, Cripinus and Agrippa conjured the spirits, and by whatever else thou mayest be conquered, that you will yield obedience to me, N.N. the same as Isaac did to Abraham, and appear before me, N.N. this instant, in the beautiful, mild, human form of a youth, and bring what I desire. (This the conjuror must name).

The most useful ministering arch angels of this seal are the following with their Hebrew verbis revelatis Citatiori divinitus coactivis: Uriel, Arael, Zacharael, Gabriel, Raphael, Theoska, Zywolech, Hemohon, Yhael, Tuwahel, Donahan, Sywaro, Samohayl, Zowanus, Ruweno Ymoeloh, Hahowel, Tywael. The particularly great secret and special use of this seal is that if this seal is buried in the earth, where treasures exist, they will come to the surface of themselves, without any presence during a full moon.

THE MYSTERY OF THE SECOND SEAL

The Name is True Seal of the Choir of Hosts or Dominations of the Ministering Angels

CONJURATION

I, N.N., a servant of God, desire, call upon and conjure thee, Spirit Phuel, by the Holy Messengers and all the Disciples of the Lord, by the four Holy Evangelists and the three Holy Men of God and by the most terrible and most holy words Abriel, Fibriel, Zada, Zaday, Zarabo, Laragola, Lavaterium, Laroyol, Zay, Zagin, Labir, Lya, Adeo, Deus, Alon, Abay, Alos, Pieus, Ehos, Mihi, Uini, Mora, Zorad, and by those holy words, that thou come and appear before me, N.N., in a beautiful human form, and bring me what I desire. (This the conjuror must name.)

This Seal from the Choir of the Dominationen, or Hosts, the following are the most useful: Aha, Rosh, Habu, Aromicha, Lemar, Patteny, Hamya, Azoth, Hayozer, Karohel, Wezynna, Patecha, Tehom. The special secret of this seal is that if a man carries this Seal with him, it will bring him great fortune and blessing; it is therefore called the truest and highest Seal of Fortune.

THE MYSTERY OF THE THIRD SEAL

Seal of the Ministering Throne Angels

CONJURATION

I, N.N., a servant of God, desire, call upon thee, and conjure thee Tehor, by all the Holy Angels and Arch Angels, by the holy Michael, the holy Gabriel, Raphael, Uriel, Thronus, Dominationes principalis, virtutes, Cherubim et Seraphim, and with unceasing voice I cry, Holy, Holy, Holy, is the Lord God of Sabaoth, and by the most terrible words: Soah, Sother, Emmanuel, Hdon, Amathon, Mathay, Adonai, Eei, Eli, Eloy, Zoag, Dios, Anath, Tafa, Uabo, Tetragramaton, Aglay, Josua, Jonas, Caplie, Caphas. Appear before me, N.N., in a mild and human form, and do what I desire. (This the conjuror must name.)

The ministering Throne Angels of this Seal are the following: Theom, Haseha, Amarzyom, Schawayt, Chuscha, Zawar, Yahel. La hehor, Adoyahel, Schimuel Achusaton, Schaddyl, Chamyl, Parymel, Chayo. The special secret of this Throne is that by carrying this Seal with you will cause you to be very agreeable and much beloved, and will also defeat all your enemies.

THE MYSTERY OF THE FOURTH SEAL

Seal of the Ministering Cherubim and Seraphim with their Characteristics

CONJURATION

I, N.N., a servant of God, call upon thee, desire and conjure thee, O Spirit Anoch, by the wisdom of Solomon, by the obedience of Isaac, by the blessing of Abraham, by the piety of Jacob and Noe, who did not sin before God, by the serpents of Moses, and by the twelve tribes, and by the most terrible words: Dallia, Dollia, Dollion, Corfuselas, Jazy, Agzy, Ahub, Tilli, Stago, Adoth, Suna, Eoluth, Alos, Jaoth, Dilu, and by all the words through which thou canst be compelled to appear before me in a beautiful, human form, and give what I desire. (This the conjuror must name.)

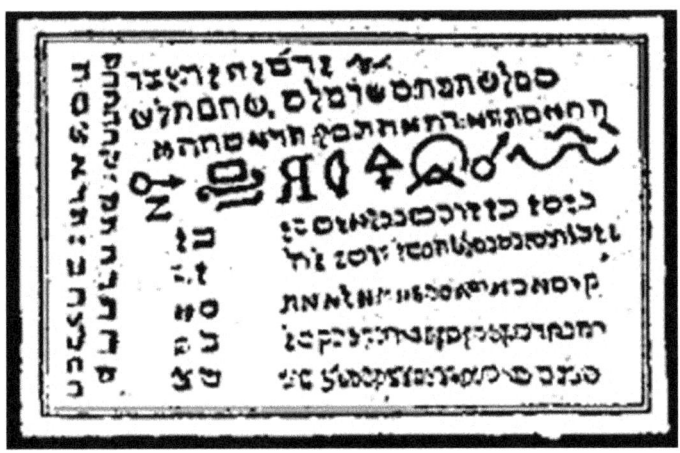

The most obliging ministering Cherubim and Seraphim of this Seal, are the following with their Hebrew calling: Anoch, Sewachar, Chaylon, Esor, Yaron, Oseny, Yagelor, Ehym, Maakyel, Echad, Yalyon, Yagar, Ragat, Ymmat, Chabalym, Schadym.

The special secret of this Seal is that to carry this Seal upon the body will save a person from all misery, and give the greatest fortune and long life.

THE MYSTERY OF THE FIFTH SEAL

Seal of the Angels of Power

CONJURATION

I, N.N., a servant of God, call upon thee, desire and conjure thee, Spirit Scheol, through the most holy appearance in the flesh of Jesus Christ, by his most holy birth and circumcision, by his sweating of blood in the Garden, by the lashes he bore, by his bitter sufferings and death, by his Resurrection, Ascension and the sending of the Holy Spirit as a comforter, and by the most dreadful words: Dai, Deorum, Ellas, genio Sophiel, Zophiel, Canoei, Elmiach, Richol, Hoamiach, Jerazol, Vohal, Daniel, Hasios, Tomaisch, Sannul, Damamlach, Sanul, Damabiath, and by those words through which thou canst be conquered, that thou appear before me in a beautiful, human form, and fulfil what I desire. (This must be named by the conjuror.)

The most serviceable Angels of Power are the following: Schoel, Hael, Sephiroth, Thamy, Schamayl, Yeehah, Holyl, Yomelo, Hadlam, Mazbaz, Elohaym.

The special secret of this Seal is that if this Seal be laid upon the sick in full, true faith, it will restore him, if he has not lived the full number of his days. Therefore, it is called the Seal of Power.

THE MYSTERY OF THE SIXTH SEAL

The Seal of the Power Angels are Potestatum over the Angels and Spirits of all the Elements

CONJURATION

I, N.N., a servant of God, desire, call upon and conjure thee, Spirit Alymon, by the most dreadful words, Sather, Ehomo, Geno, Poro, Jehovah, Elohim, Volnah, Denach, Alonlam, Ophiel, Zophiel, Sophiel, Habriel, Eloha, Alesimus, Dileth, Melohim, and by all the holiest words through which thou canst be conquered, that thou appear before me in a mild, beautiful human form, and fulfil what I command thee, so surely as God will come to judge the living and the dead. Fiat, Fiat, Fiat.

The most obedient Angels of Power, seu Potestates, are the following four elements: Schunmyel, Alymon, Mupiel, Symnay,

Semanglaf, Taftyah, Melech, Seolam, Waed, Sezah, Safyn, Kyptip, Taftyarohel, Aeburatiel, Anyam, Bymnam. This is the mystery or Seal of the Might-Angels. The peculiar Arcanum of this Seal of the Mighty is that if a man wears this seal in bed, he will learn what he desires to know through dreams and visions.

THE MYSTERY OF THE SEVENTH SEAL

Seal of the Angels of the Seven Planets and Spirits

CONJURATION

I, N.N., a servant of God, call upon, desire, and conjure thee, Ahael, Banech, by the most holy words Agios, (Tetr.,) Eschiros, Adonai, Alpha et Omega, Raphael, Michael, Uriel, Schmaradiel, Zaday, and by all the known names of Almighty God, by whatever thou, Ahael, canst be compelled, that thou appear before me, in a human form, and fulfil what I desire. Fiat, Fiat, Fiat. (This must be named by the conjuror.)

The most obedient Angels and Spirits of this Seal of the Seven Planets are the following: Ahaeb, Baneh, Yeschnath, Hoschiah, Betodah, Leykof, Yamdus, Zerenar, Sahon. This Seal, when laid upon the treasure earth, or when placed within the works of a mine, will reveal all the precious contents of the mine.

THE SEVENTH BOOK OF MOSES

THE TWELVE TABLES OF THE SPIRITS

THE FIRST TABLE OF THE SPIRITS OF THE AIR

Conjuration

Jehovah Father, Deus Adonay Elohe, I cite Thee through Jehovah. Deus Schadday, Eead, I conjure Thee through Adonay.

To carry upon the person the First Table of the Spirits of the Air, who areas quick as thought to help, will relieve the wearer from all necessity.

THE SECOND TABLE OF THE SPIRITS OF FIRE

Conjuration

Aha, I conjure Thee (Tetragrammaton) Aha by Eheye, * by Ihros, Eheye, by Agla Aysch, Jehovah, conjure I Thee, that thou appear unto me.

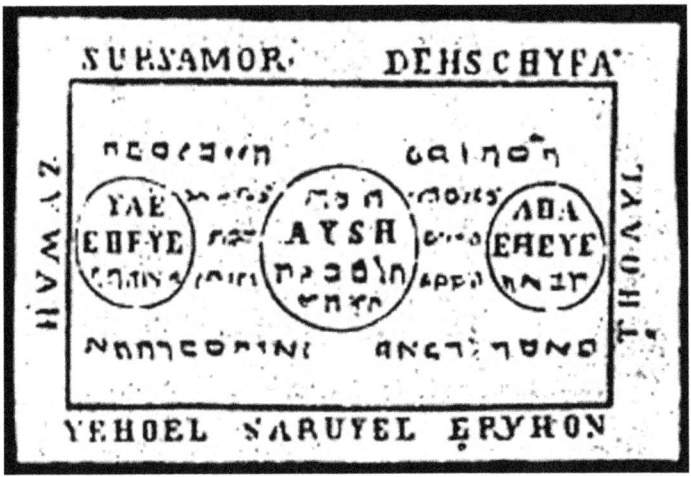

THE THIRD TABLE OF THE SPIRITS OF WATER

Conjuration

I call upon and command thee Chananya by God Tetragrammaton Eloh. I conjure Thee Yeschaijah by Alpha and Omega, and Thou art compelled through Adonai.

The Third Table brings great fortune by water, and its spirits will amply supply the treasures of the deep.

THE FOURTH TABLE OF THE SPIRITS OF THE EARTH

Conjuration

I, N.N., command Thee, Awijel, by Otheos as also by Elmez through Agios. I, N.N., a servant of God, conjure Thee, Ahenatos Elijon, as also Adon was cited and called Zebaoth.

This Fourth Table will give the treasures of the earth, if it be laid in the earth. Its spirits will give the treasures of the earth at all times.

THE FIFTH TABLE OF SATURN

Conjuration

I, N.N., order, command and conjure Thee Sazlij, by Agios, Sedul, by Sother, Veduij, by Sabaot, Sove, Amonzion * Adoij, by Helohim, Jaho, by the Veritas Jehovah * Kawa, Alha, natos that ye must appear before me in human form, so truly as Daniel overcame and conquered Baal. Fiat, Fiat, Fiat.

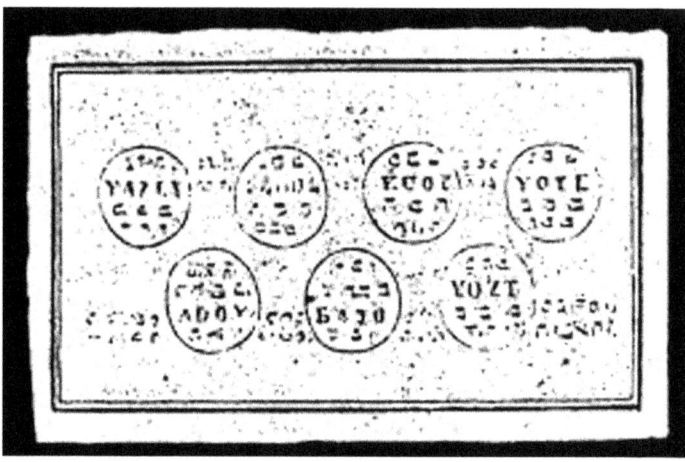

The Spirits of the Fifth Table of Saturn will serve in everything according to wish. Their Table will bring good luck in play(games of chance).

THE SIXTH TABLE OF JUPITER

Conjuration

I conjure Thee, Spirit Ofel, by Alpha and Omega, Lezo and Yschirios * Ohin Ission * Niva, by Tetragrammaton, Zeno, by Peraclitus * Ohel, by Orlenius, Lima, by Agla *, that ye will obey and appear before me and fulfil my desire, thus in and through the name Elion, which Moses named. Fiat, fiat, fiat.

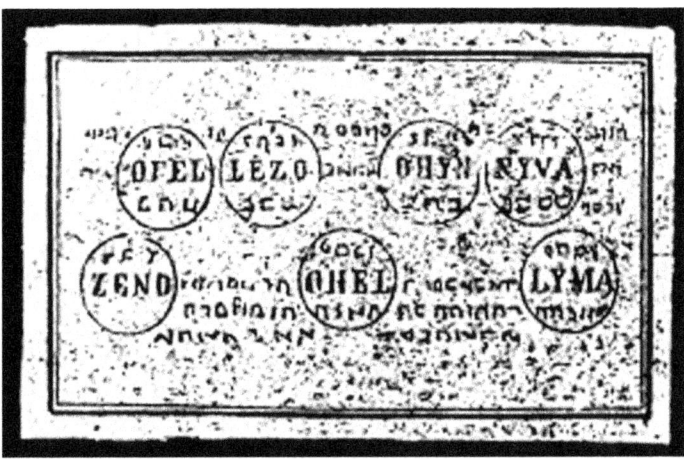

The Sixth Table of Jupiter assists in overcoming lawsuits, disputes, and in winning at play or games of chance. Their spirits are at all times ready to render assistance.

THE SEVENTH TABLE OF MARS

Conjuration

I, N.N., cite Thee, Spirit Emol, by Deus Sachnaton * Luil, by Acumea * Luiji, by Ambriel *, Tijlaij, by Ehos *, by Jeha, by Zora * Ageh, by Awoth, * that you appear before me in a beautiful, human form, and accomplish my desire, thus truly in and through the anepobeijaron, which Aaron heard and which was prepared for him. Fiat, fiat, fiat.

The Seventh Seal of Mars brings good fortune. In case of quarrels the Spirits of Mars will help you.

THE EIGHTH TABLE OF THE SUN

Conjuration

I, N.N., conjure Thee, Wrjch by Dalia ⊠ Jka, by Doluth *, Auet, by Dilu * Veal, by Anub ⊠ Meho, by Igfa * Ymij, by Eloij * that Ye appear before my so true Zebaoth, who was named by Moses, and all the rivers in Egypt were turned into blood.

THE NINTH TABLE OF VENUS

Conjuration

Reta, Kijmah, Yamb, Yheloruvesopijhael, I call upon Thee, Spirit Awel, through God Tetragrammaton, Uhal, by Pomamiach that you will obey my commands and fulfil my desires. Thus truly in and through the name of Esercheije, which Moses named, and upon which followed hail, the like of which was not known since the beginning of the world. Fiat, fiat, fiat.

The Ninth Table of the Spirits of Venus makes one beloved in all respects and makes secrets known through dreams. Its spirits also assist liberally in all kinds of business.

THE TENTH TABLE OF MERCURY

Conjuration

Petasa, Ahor, Havaashar, N. N., cites Thee Spirit Yloij * through God, God Adonaij ⊠ Ymah, through God Tetragrammaton ⊠ Rawa, through God Emanuel * Ahaij, through Athanatos ⊠ that Thou appear before me as truly in and through the name of Adonai, which Moses mentioned, and there appeared grasshoppers. fiat, fiat, fiat.

The Tenth Table of the Spirits of Mercury gives wealth in Chemistry. These spirits contribute treasures of the mines.

THE ELEVENTH TABLE OF THE SPIRITS

Conjuration

I, N.N., cite Thee, Spirit Yhaij, by El, Yvaij, by Elohim, Ileh, by Elho * Kijlij, by Zebaoth, Taijn Iseij, by Tetragrammaton, Jeha, by Zadaij * Ahel, by Agla that you will obey my orders, as truly in and through the name Schemesumatie, upon which Josua called, and the sun stood still in its course. Fiat, fiat, fiat.

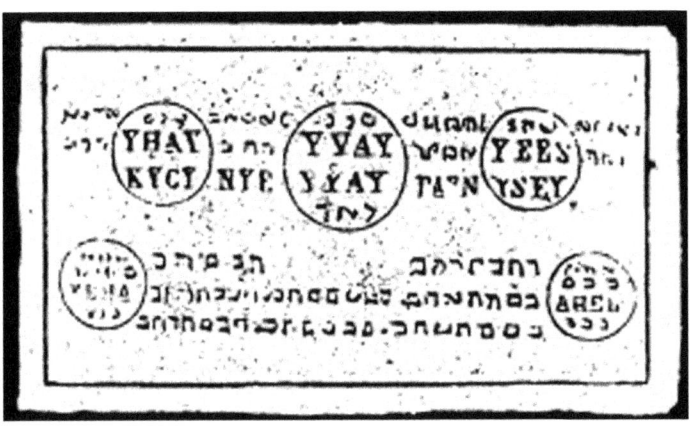

The Eleventh Table gives good luck and fortune. Its spirits give the treasures of the sea.

THE TWELFTH TABLE OF THE SCHEMHAMFORASCH

(On All Spirits of White and Black Magic)

Conjuration

I, N.N., cite and conjure Thee, Spirit of Schehamforasch, by all the seventy-two holy names of God, that Thou appear before me and fulfil my desire, as truly in and through the name Emanuel, which the three youths Sadrach, Mijsach, and Abednegro sung in the fiery furnace from which they were released. Fiat, fiat, fiat.

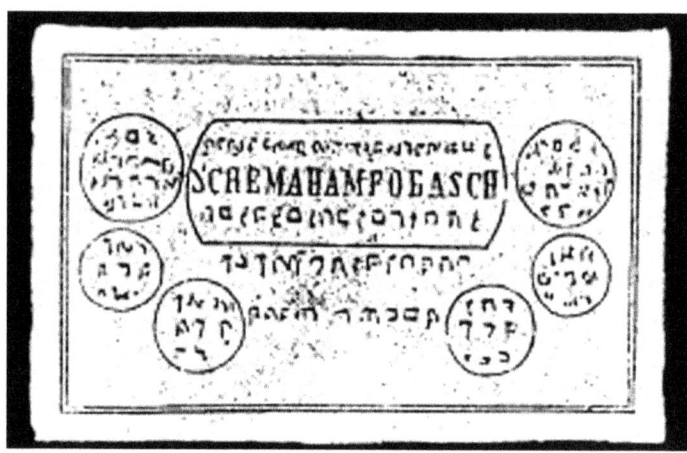

This Twelfth Table when laid upon the Table or Seal of the Spirits will compel them to appear immediately, and to serve in all things.

THE MINISTERING FORMULAS OR MYSTERIES

The following formulas must be cited by the Twelfth Table during a sun or lunar eclipse:

Astarte, Salomonis familiarum III, Eegum
Spirit of Water, Spirit of Air, Spirit of Earth
Astoreth in Palestina familiari
Schaddaij, Driffon, Agrippa, Magaripp.
Azijelzm, Sinna, familiarum IV, Buch Regum
Schijwin * Aimeh, Chanije, Cijbor
Bealherith ijud Judicum IX, XIII
Adola, Eloheij, Umijchob Channanijah
Adramelech zu Sepharavaijm, Familiaris
Yhaij, Vvaij, Yles, Kijgij
Nisroch, Regis Serucheril Assijris familiaris
Jehuel, Sarwiel, Urikon, Thoijil

Asijma, Virorum Emach familiaris
Barechel, Jomar, Ascher, Uwula

GENERATION SEAL

This Generation Seal, also known as Moloch familiarum or Ammonitarium Ministering Spirits, makes its spirits obedient in all services. At the time of Citation, it must be written on parchment and held in the right hand, but it must not be read.

EXTRACT FROM THE MAGICAL KABALA

The Citation-Formulas contained in this book must only be pronounced in the Hebrew language, and in no other. In any other language they have no power whatever, and the Master can never be sure of their effects. For all these words and forms were thus pronounced by the Great Spirit, and have power only in the Hebrew language.

BREASTPLATE OF MOSES

The Hebrew inscriptions within the seal are pronounced as follows:

JEHOVA, ASER EHEJE CETHER ELEION EHEJE

Their meaning is as follows:

The Most High, whom no eye hath seen, nor tongue spoke; the Spirit which did great acts and performed great wonders. The

Words of the Breastplate and the Helmet pronounced mean Holiness.

HELMET OF MOSES AND AARON

The Hebrew inscriptions are to be pronounced as follows:

HIEBEL MARE ACTITAS BARNE DONENE ARIAERCH

These are the names which the old Egyptians used instead of the unutterable name of Asser Criel, and are called the "Fire of God," and "Strong Rock of Faith." Whoever wears them on his person will not die a sudden death.

BREASTPLATE OF AARON

The inscriptions on the seal are to be pronounced as follows:

SADAJAI AMARA ELON HEJIANA VANANEL PHENATON EBCOEL MERAI

That is, a Prince of Miens, the other leads to Jehova. Through this, God spoke to Moses.

MAGICAL LAW OF MOSES

The inscriptions on the seal are to be read as follows:

AILA HIMEL ADONAIJ AMARA ZEBAOTH CADAS YESERAIJE HARALIUS

These words are terrible, and will assemble devils or spirits, or they will cause the dead to appear.

THE INSCRIPTION ON THE CHALICE OF HOLINESS

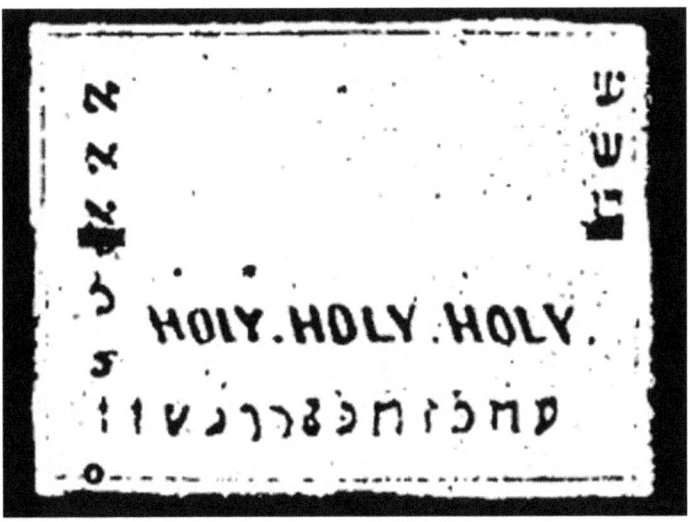

The inscriptions on the seal are to be read as follows:

ELIAON JOENA EBREEL ELOIJELA AIJEL AGONI SOCHADON

These words are great and mighty. They are names of the Creator and the characters on the Ark of the Covenant.

CONJURATION OF ELEAZAR, THE SON OF AARON

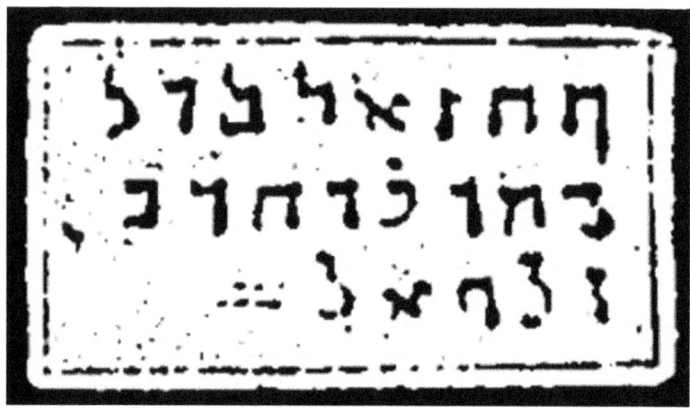

The inscriptions on the seal are to be read as follows:

UNIEL DILATAN SADAI PANEIM USAMIGRAS CALIPHOS SASNA SOIM JALAPH

These names, if anyone desires to accomplish anything through the four elements or any other things connected therewith, will prove effective, but they cannot be translated into English.

DISMISSION OF ELEAZAR, THE SON OF AARON

The inscriptions on the seal are to be read as follows:

LEAY YLI ZIARITE ZELOHABE ET NEGORAMY ZIEN LATEBM DAMA MECHA RA METI OZIRA

Through this dismission all things dissolve into nothing.

CITATION OF GERMUTHSAI OR LEVIATHAN

The inscriptions on the seal are to be read as follows:

LAGUMEN EMANUEL THEREFORI MECHELAG LAIGEL YAZI ZAZAEL

With these names Eleazar bound and unbound the spirits of the air.

DISMISSION OF LEVIATHAN

The inscriptions on the seal are to be read as follows:

MALCOH, SADAIJ, CUBOR DAMABIAH MENKIE LEJABEL MANIAH IJEJAVAI

That is, Strong, Might spirit of hell, go back into thine own Works, in the name of Jehova.

BALAAM'S SORCERY

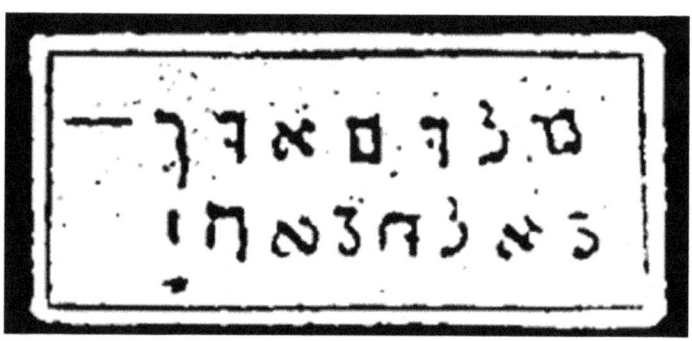

The inscriptions on this seal are to be read as follows:

MELOCH, HEL ALOKIM TIPHRET HOD JESATH

This brings vengeance upon enemies, and must not be disregarded because it contains the names of the Seven Tables of the Covenant.

EGYPT

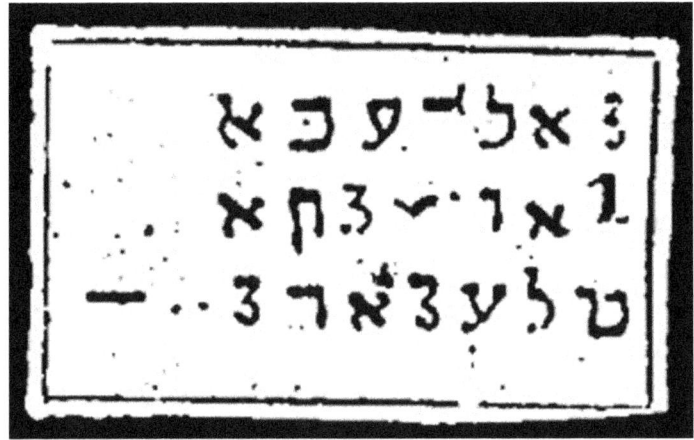

The inscriptions on the seal are to be read as follows:

TANABTIAN AINATEN PAGNIJ AIJOLO ASNIA HICHAIFALE MATAE HABONR HIJCERO

With these words Moses spake to the sorcerers in Egypt. They signify: "The Lord appeared to his servant in the fire, to seal the earth in its four quarters, and the nether earth."

CONJURATION OF THE LAWS OF MOSES

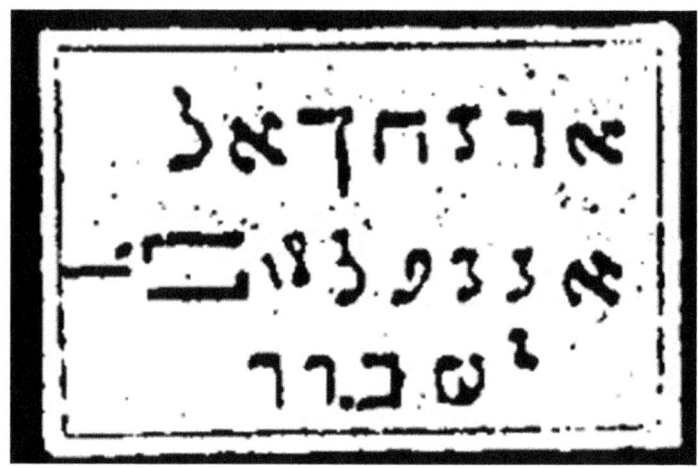

The inscription on the seal must be read as follows;

AIJCON DUNSANAS PETHANIR THRIJGNIR IJON CIJNA NATER LAVIS PISTOIN

If you wish to pronounce these words you must fast for three days, and you can perform wonders therewith. They cannot be translated on account of the Hebrew characters.

GENERAL CITATION OF MOSES ON ALL SPIRITS

The inscriptions on the seal are to be read as follows:

ELION GOEUA ADONAIJ CADAS EBREEL, ELOIL ELA AGIEL, AIJONI SACHADON, ESSUSELAS ELOHIM, DELIION JAU ELIJULA, DELIA JARI ZAZAEL PALIEMAO UMIEL, ONALA DILATUM SADATJ, ALMA JOD JAEL THAMA

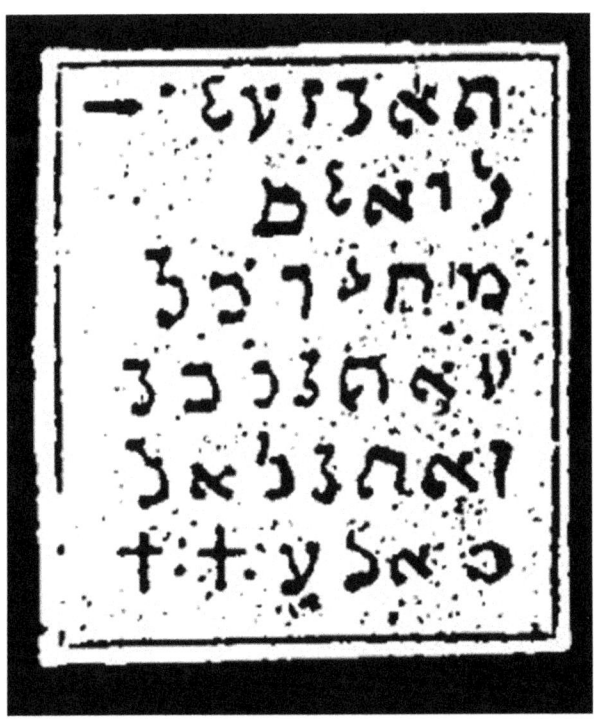

This citation is great and mighty. They are the names of the Creator, and the names of the two Cherubim on the Mercy Seat, Zarall and Jael.

DISMISSION OF MOSES

The inscriptions on this seal are to be read as follows:

WASZEDIM BACHANDA HEZANHAD JEHOV ELOHIM ASSER EHOIE ZALIM

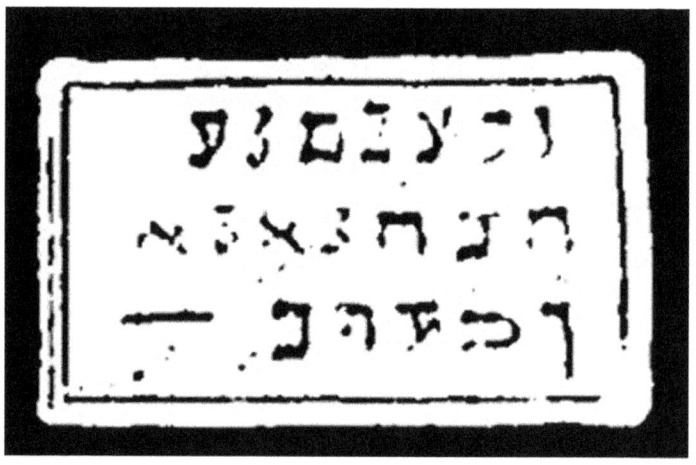

GENERAL CITATION OF MOSES ON ALL SPIRITS

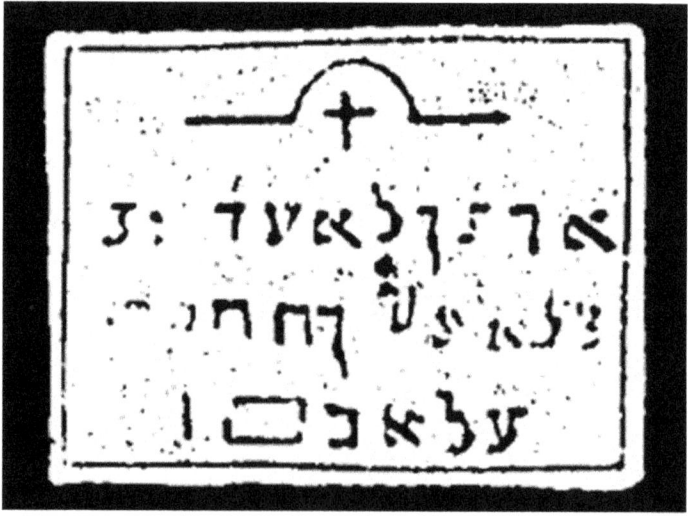

The inscriptions on the seal are to be read as follows:

AHEZERAIJE COMITEJON SEDE LEJI THOMOS SASMAGATA BIJ UL IJCOS JOUA ELOIJ ZAWAIJM

These are the high and powerful utterances that Moses employed in the awakening of the Leviathan, in order to compel him to serve his Lord. The first cannot be uttered and was used by the first inhabitants of earth as a mighty lord. The whole is good, but not everyone can obtain it in perfection without severe discipline.

CHARACTERS ON THE LEFT SIDE OF THE ARK OF THE COVENANT OF THE MOST HIGH

CHARACTERS ON THE RIGHT SIDE OF THE ARK OF THE COVENANT OF THE MOST HIGH

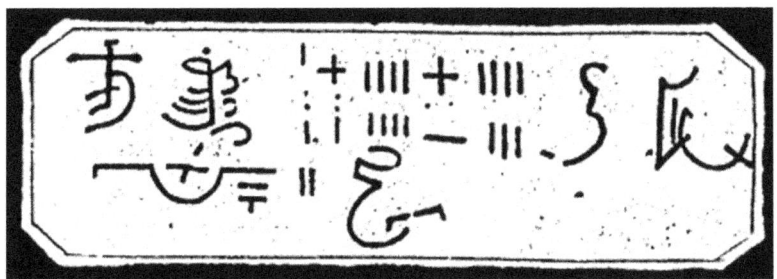

Hear, Oh Israel, the Lord our God is God alone.

CONJURED SPIRIT APPEARS ON A PILLAR OF FIRE

The inscriptions on the seal are to be said as follows:

AFFABIJ ZIEN, JERAMIJE LATABI DAMAJESANO NOIJ LIJOIJ LEAIJ GLIJ EIJLOIJ LIECLE LOATE ELI ELI MECHARAMETHIJ RIJIBISAS SA FU AZIRA REACHA

The Citation names the twelve evil spirits of man, through the help of the Father, of the Hebrew Eli. It is terrible.

CONJURED SPIRIT APPEARS ON A PILLAR OF CLOUDS

The inscriptions on the seal are to be read as follows:

KAHAI CONOR ANUHEC ZELOHAE ZOLE HEBEI EDE NEGO RANEIJ HAHABE GIZAON

Appendix to the General Citation of Moses on All Spirits

We, N.N., in this circle, conjure and cite this spirit Fatenovenia, with all his adherents, to appear here in this spot, to fulfil our desires, in the name of the three holy angels, Schomajen Sheziem, Roknion Averam, Kandile, Brachat Chaijdalic, Ladabas, Labul, Raragil, Bencul, in the name of God. Amen.

THREE NEW SIGNS WITH FROGS, LICE AND PESTILENCE

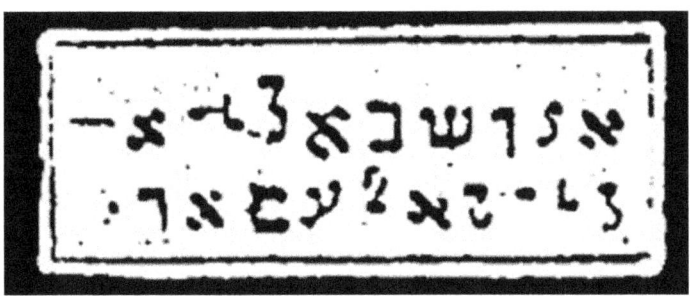

The inscriptions on the seal to be read as follows:

ABLAN, AGEISTAN, ZORATAN JURAN, NONDIERAS PORTAEPHIAS POGNIJ AIZAMAI

THREE NEW SIGNS WITH CATTLE, PESTILENCE, BLACK SMALL-POX AND HAIL

The inscriptions on the seal are to be read as follows:

ARARITA ZAIJN THANAIN, MIORATO RAEPI SATHONIK PETHANIT CASTAS LUCAS CALBERA NATUR SIGAIM

SIGNS OF GRASSHOPPERS AND DARKNESS

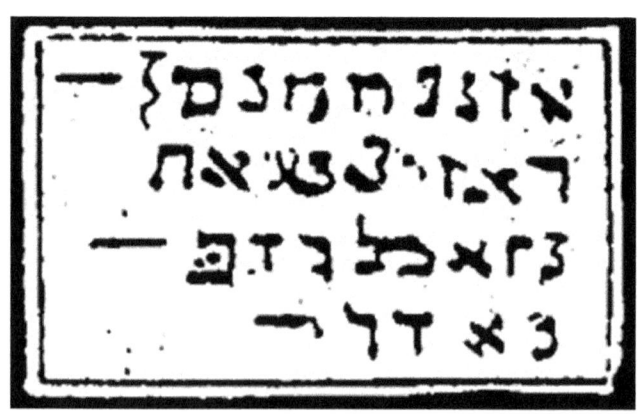

The inscriptions on the seal are to be said as follows:

HASSADAY HAYLOES, LUCASIM ELAYH JACIHAGA, YOININO, SEPACTICAS BARNE LUD CASTY:

THE SPIRIT APPEARS IN THE BURNING BUSH

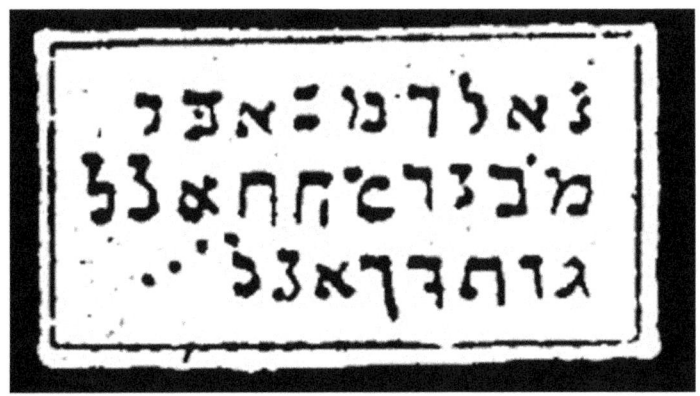

The inscriptions on the seal are to be read as follows:

BABA CUCI HIEBU ZIADHI ELENEHET NA VEAN VIE ACHYA SALNA

The spirit which appears here is God himself.

MOSES CHANGES THE STAFF INTO A SERPENT

The inscriptions on the seal are to be read as follows:

MICRATA RAEPI SATHONIK PETHANISCH, PISTAN IJTTINGE HIJGATIGN IJGHUZIAN TEMGARONUSNIA CASTAS LACIAS ASTAS IJECON CIJNA CALTERA CAPHAS

MOSES CHANGES WATER INTO BLOOD

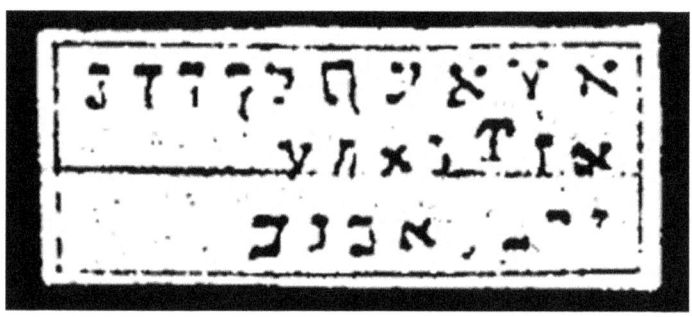

The inscriptions on the seal are to be read as follows:

ABEN AGLA MANDEL SLOP SIEHAS MALIM HAJATH HAJADOSCH IJONEM, CEDAS EBREEL AMPHIA, DEMISRAEL MUELLE LEAGIJNS AMANIHA

EXTRACT FROM THE TRUE CLAVICULA OF SOLOMON AND THE GIRDLE OF AARON

This was bequeathed as a testament to all the wise magicians, which all the old Fathers possessed and employed, to have and fulfill all things through the illustrious power of the mighty God

Jehovah, as He, the great Monarch, gave to His creatures, who worship Him day and night with reverence and fear, who call loudly upon His name in secret, and sigh to Him as their origin, as of Him and from Him existing reasonable beings, as on the point of being involved with the pains of the elements, who strive after the highest being to and with God. To these He has given this, who will not forget Him in the pleasures of this world, who, still bearing suffering without forgetting the reality, nor the perishing lustre of the world.

PRINCIPAL CITATION ON ALL MINISTERING SPIRITS OF THE AIR AND OF EARTH, THE LIKE OF WHICH MANASSES AND SOLOMON USED AS THE TRUE KEY SOLOMONIS REGIS ISRAEL

You must stand on a prominent rock, hold a palm twig in your right hand, and wear a wreath of laurel around the temples. Then turn toward the east and say:

ALIJA LAIJA LAUMIN OTHEON!

At this time, a halo of light will surround you, and when you become aware of this light, fall upon your knees and worship. Then say in an audible voice the words inscribed in the following seal. You must speak slowly and distinctly.

ELIAM YOENA ADONAI CADUS EBREEL ELOYELA AGIEL, AYOM SACHADON OSSUSELAS ELOYM DE LIOMAR ELYNLA LELIA YAZI ZAZALL UNNEL OVELA DILATAM SADAY ALMA PANAIM ALYM CANAL DENSY USAMI YASAS CALIPI CALFAS SASNA SAFFA SADOJA AGLATA PANTOMEL AMRIEL AZIEN PHANATON SARZE PENERION YA EMANUEL JOD JALAPH AMPHIA THAN DOMIRAEL ALOWIN.

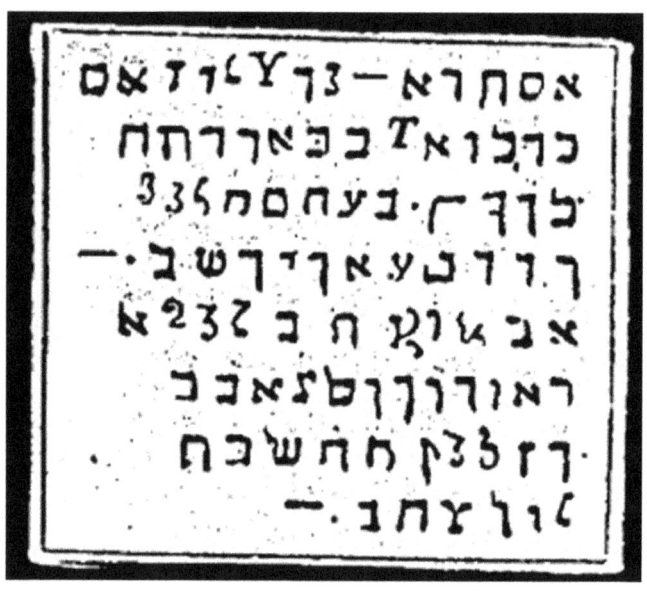

CHARACTERS

BA M N LAZIES ALA PHONFIN AGALOYES PYOL PAERTEON THESERYM. BASIMEL JAEL BARIONIA APIOLET CENET.

TREATISE SION

(The Revelation of Zion)

TRANSLATOR'S PREFACE

SINCE the Oriental transcript of this work was imperfect in many parts, the translation of it had to be taken according to the great original book, on account of the purity of its text, and, therefore, it won for itself the advantage of understanding and completing the exercises with serenity and confidence. The translator, in the meantime believes, that no one, who feels honestly called to these things, can ever be made the subject of ill-fortune, or be deceived by the wiles and deceptions of the old serpent, the inevitable fate that will and must fall to his lot under any other exorcisms, and that he may cheerfully and safely move thence. because only the angels of God will perform the service required by Him.

INTRODUCTION AND BEGINNING

The Vestibule of Entrance

The language and manuscript of this rare and eternal monument of light, and of a higher wisdom, are borrowed from the Cuthans, a tribe of the Samaritans, who were called Cuthim in the Chaldee dialect according to the Talmud, and they were so called in a spirit of derision. They were termed sorcerers because they taught in Cutha, their original place of abode, and afterward in Samaria, the Kabala or Higher Magic (Book of Kings). Caspar, Melchior and Balthazar, the chosen archpriests, are shining lights among the Eastern magicians. They were kings and teachers--the first priest-teachers of this glorious knowledge--and from these Samaritans-Cuthans, who were called Nergal according to the traditions of the Talmud, originated the Gypsies, who, through degeneracy, lost the consecration of their primordial powers.

LAWS OF ENTRANCE

1. Before you can enter the temple of consecrated light, you must purify your soul and body during thirteen days.

2. As a brother and disciple of the new covenant, or as a Christian, you must receive the Holy Sacrament for the glorification of the three kings--Caspar, Melchior and Balthasar.

3. Three holy masses must be read as often as you make use of this book in your priestly service with your intention fixed upon the three glorified kings.

4. You must provide yourself with a ram's horn, wherewith to call together the angels and spirits. This horn must be included in your intentions of the holy mass.

5. You must wear a breastplate of parchment, ten inches high and ten inches wide, inscribed with the names of the twelve apostles with the five-fold name of Schemhamforasch, in the same order that it is placed on the last leaf.

6. You must draw a circle around you upon white paper, or upon sky blue silk. Its circumference shall be thirteen feet, and at the distance of each foot, one of the following names must be written: Moseh, Messias, Aaron, Jehova, Adoni, Jesus, Christus, Caspar, Melchior, Balthasar. Al. Al. Al.

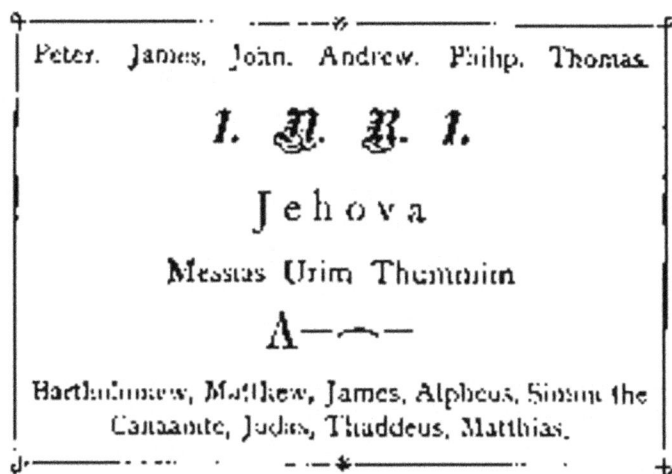

7. Between each name you must place the holy symbol of Horet: or .

8. The breastplate must be included in the intention of the holy mass.

9. Through consecration with holy three king's water and with three burning wax tapers, you must finally pronounce a benediction over this book, the horn, the breastplate, and the circle, after reading a well-selected mysterious ritual.

10. You may enter alone, or begin this great work with two companions, by day or night, but always from the first to the thirteenth of the month, and during the thirteenth day, and through the whole night of the new moon, and also during the full moon, when the three planets, Saturn, Mars and Jupiter, are visible in the heavens on the day of exorcism, either singly or together.

11. You must always stand with your face toward Zion, or toward the rising of the sun.

12. He who refuses a copy of this book, or who suppresses it or steals it, will be seized with eternal trembling like Cain, and the angels of god will depart from him.

TREATISE OF THE SIXTH BOOK OF MOSES

CHAPTER I. THE SPIRIT APPEARS UNTO MOSES IN A BURNING BUSH

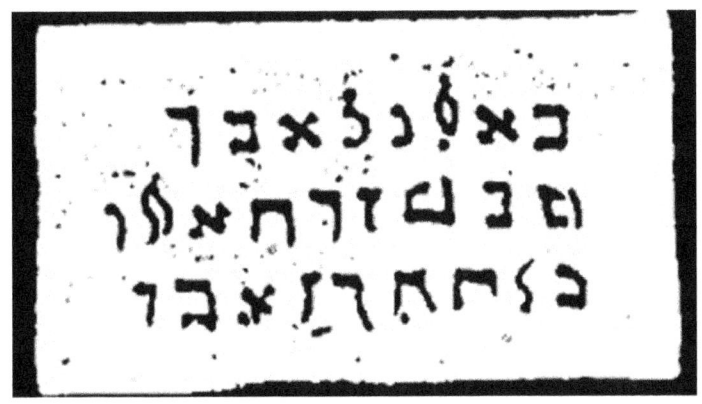

Conjuration

KALUKU! UBESU! LAWISU!--Arise and teach me.

Calls with voice and horn as instructed.

CHAPTER II. MOSES CHANGES THE STAFF INTO A SERPENT

Conjuration

TUWISU! KAWISU! LAWISU!--Arise and change this staff into a serpent.

Calls with voice and horn as instructed.

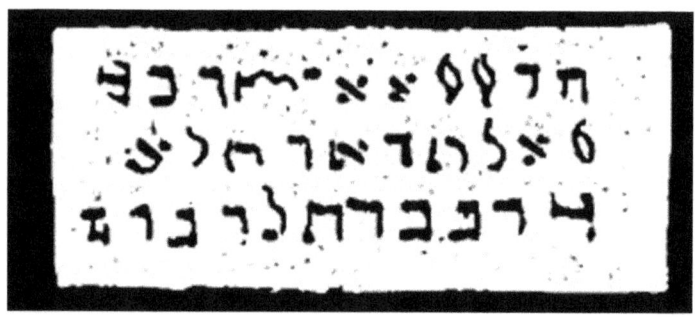

CHAPTER III. MOSES CHANGES WATER INTO BLOOD

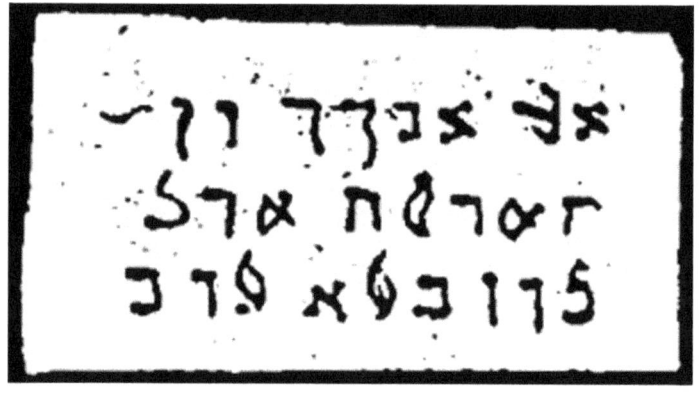

Conjuration

AKAUATIU! TUWALU! LABATU!--Arise and change this water into blood.

Calls with voice and horn as instructed.

CHAPTER IV. THREE NEW SIGNS WITH FROGS, MICE, LICE AND SIMILAR VERMIN

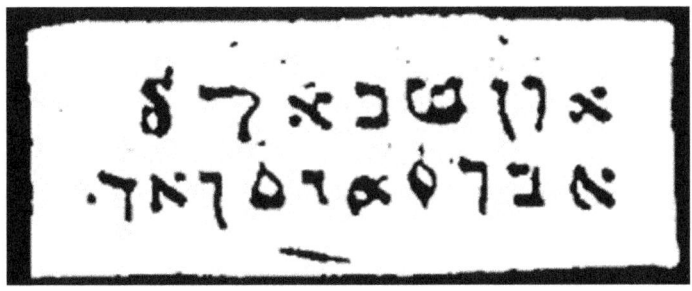

Conjuration

ADUS! BAACHUR! ARBU! ULU!--Frogs, mice, lice and similar vermin arise in our service.

CHAPTER V. THREE SIGNS OF CATTLE PESTILENCE, BLACK SMALL POX AND HAIL

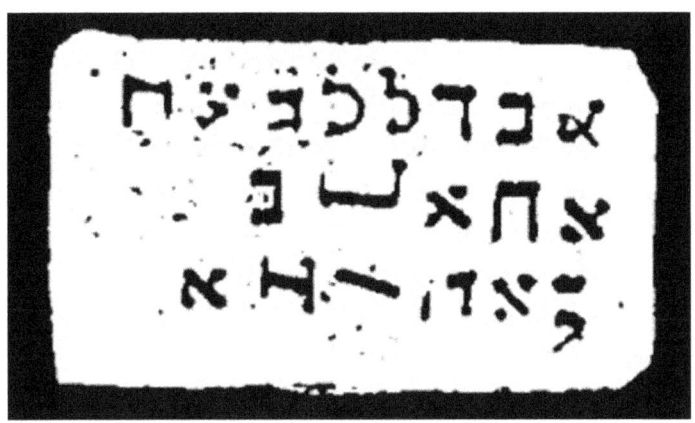

Conjuration

ABULL, BAA!--Pestilence, black smallpox and hail, arise in our service.

CHAPTER VI. THREE SIGNS WITH GRASSHOPPERS AND DARKNESS

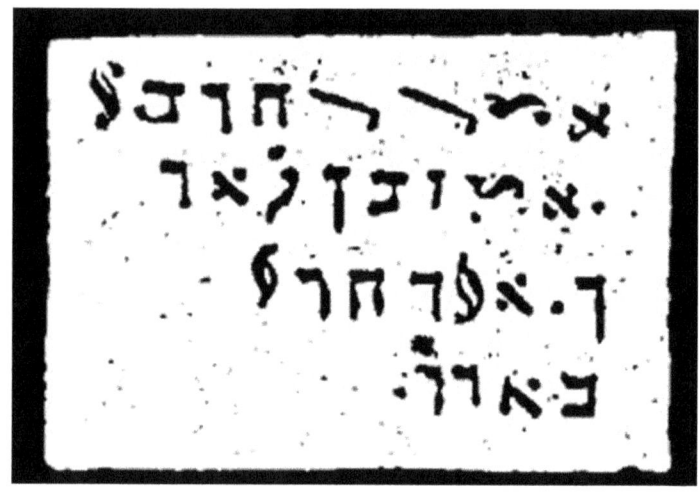

Conjuration

ARDUSI! DALUSI!--Grasshoppers, darkness, arise in our service.

These are the plagues which the Cuthians often employed in their exorcisms for punishment.

CHAPTER VII. GENERAL CITATION OF MOSES ON ALL SPIRITS

Conjuration

ADULAL! ABULAL! LEBUSI!--Arise and bring before me the spirit N.

Calls with voice and horn as instructed.

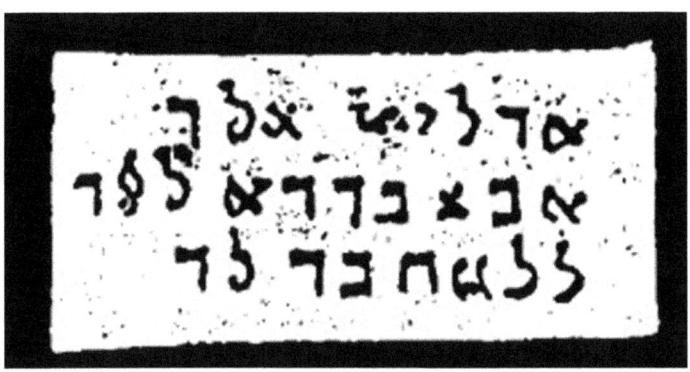

THE PENTAGON OR OMNIPOTENT FIVE CORNERS

This mysterious figure must be written before the conjuration, in the open air and on the ground, with consecrated chalk or with the index finger of the right hand dipped in holy three-king's water, the same as it is written on the illustration, but each line must be thirteen feet in length. The conjuror then kneels in the center of the star, facing east with head uncovered, and calls out thirteen times, with great faith and fervor, the names of the three kings, Caspar, Melchior and Balthasar. He then calls out, with equal sentiment, the most sacred name of Elohim, 375 times. This conjuration can only take place during the first three days or nights of the new or full moon, or when Saturn, Mars and Jupiter are visible in the heavens, as established in the Laws of Entrance.

TREATISE OF THE SEVENTH BOOK OF MOSES

CHAPTER I. THE SPIRIT APPEARS IN A PILLAR OF FIRE BY NIGHT

Conjuration

TALUBSI! LATUBUSI! KALUBUSI! ALUSI!--Arise and bring me the pillar of Fire that I may see.

The name of each angel must be called out three times to the four quarters of the earth, first with the voice, then with the horn.

CHAPTER II. THE SPIRIT APPEARS IN A PILLAR OF CLOUD BY DAY

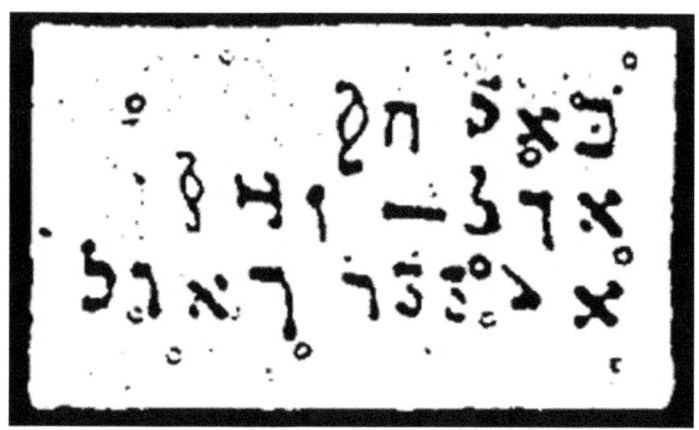

Conjuration

BUAL! COME! AUL! ARISE! TUBO! COME! WEGULO! ARISE!

The blowing of the horn must be repeated.

CHAPTER III. BALAAM'S SORCERY

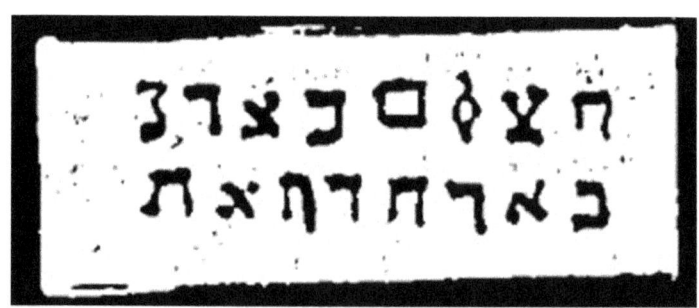

Conjuration

ONU, BASCHBA, NISCHOAZ HUERETZ--In the name of God I conjure the earth.

CHAPTER IV. EGYPT

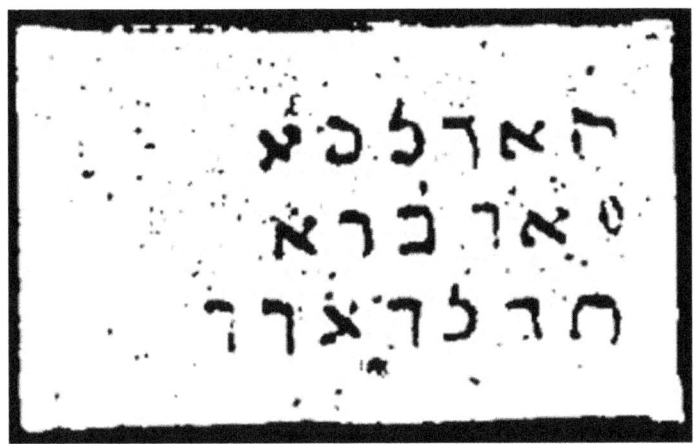

Conjuration of Three Angels

GEBRIL! MEACHUEL! NESANEL!--By the lamp of the threefold eternal light, let N.N. appear before me.

Three calls with the voice and three with the horn.

CHAPTER V. CONJURATION OF THE LAWS OF MOSES

Conjuration

KEISEHU, NISCHBA, LAWEMSO--How to be God, so swarest Thou to our parents.

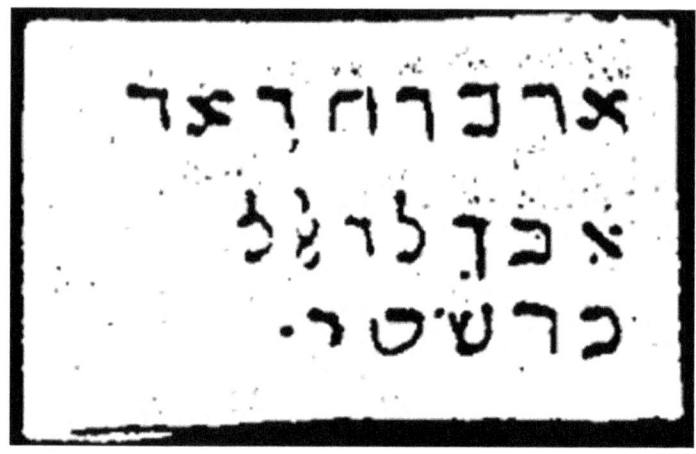

Prayer

Eternal of Eternals! Jehovah of Light, Adonai of Truth! Messiah of the All Merciful! Jesus Christ the Beloved and All Redemption and Love! Thou hast said: Who seeth me seeth also the Father. Father, eternal Father of the old and new convenants. Triune Father, Triune Son, Triune Spirit, our Father, I beseech and conjure Thee by the eternal words of Thy eternal truth.

Now read the 17th chapter of John or Jesus' prayer.

Closing Prayer of the Conjuration of the Law

Eternal God Jehovah, Thou hast said: Ask and it shall be given you. I pray that Thou mayest hear Thy servants Caspar, Melchior and Balthasar, the archpriest of Thy fountain of light! I pray that I thou mayest bid thine angels to purify me from all sin; that they may breathe upon me in love, and that they may cover me with the shadow of their wings. Send them down! This is my prayer in peace!

CHAPTER VI. GENERAL CITATION OF MOSES ON ALL SPIRITS

* CHAPTER VII. GENERAL CITATION OF MOSES ON ALL SPIRITS

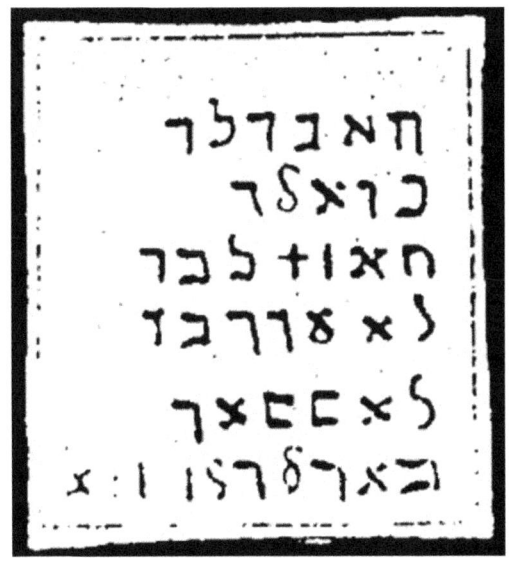

Conjuration

TUBATLU! BUALU! TULATU! LABUS! UBLISI!--Let there appear and bring before me the spirit of N.N.

Each of these five omnipotent angels must be called three times toward the four quarters of the world, first with the voice then with the horn, to make a total of six calls.

DISMISSAL OF MOSES

Conjuration

UBELUTUSI! KADUKULITI! KEBUTZI!--Take away from my Presence the spirit of N.N.

Twelve calls with the voice and twelve calls with the horn for each name.

* CHAPTER VII. CONJURATION OF ELEAZAR

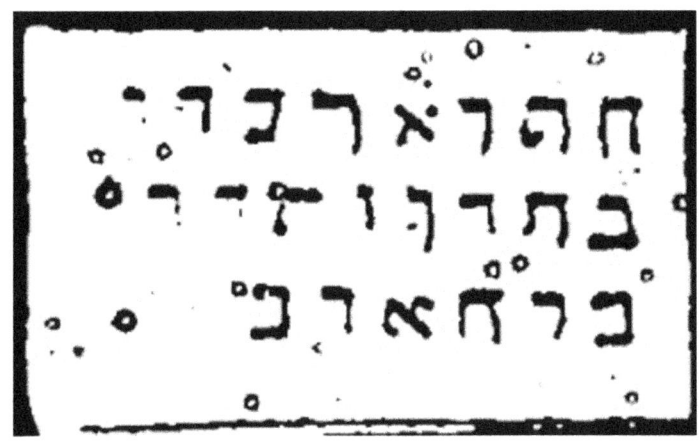

DUWATU, BUWATIE, BEMAIM--I come to you on the water! Bring me up N.N.!

DISMISSAL OF ELEAZAR

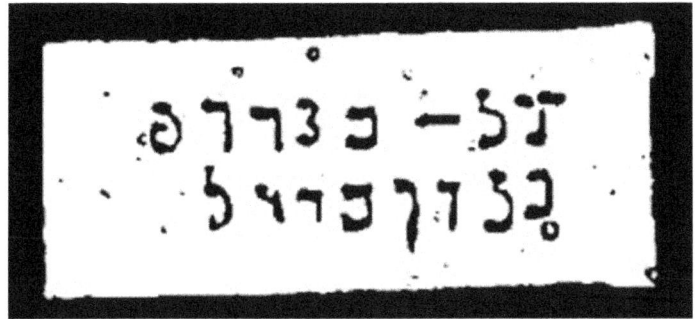

Conjuration

ORUM, BOLECTN, UBAJOM--Cursed by night and by day!

CHAPTER VIII. CITATION OF QUERNITHAY OR LEVIATHAN

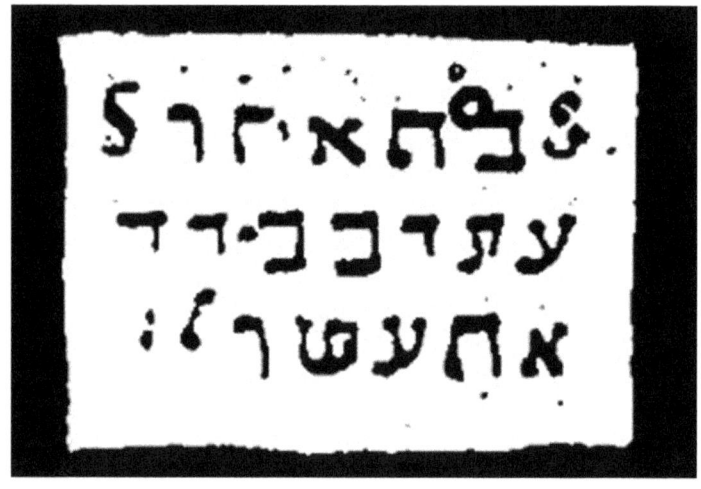

Conjuration

ELUBATEL, EBUHUEL, ATUESUEL!

Each name must be repeated three times. These, as well as the following invocations, contain only the peculiar names of the angels of omnipotence who will permit the conjured spirits to appear, or will compel them to appear by force.

DISMISSAL

Conjuration

I beseech thee, angel Elubatel, conduct N.N. {name of spirit} from my presence.

Each angel's name must be pronounced three times with the voice and three times the horn must be blown, each time towards the four quarters of the earth.

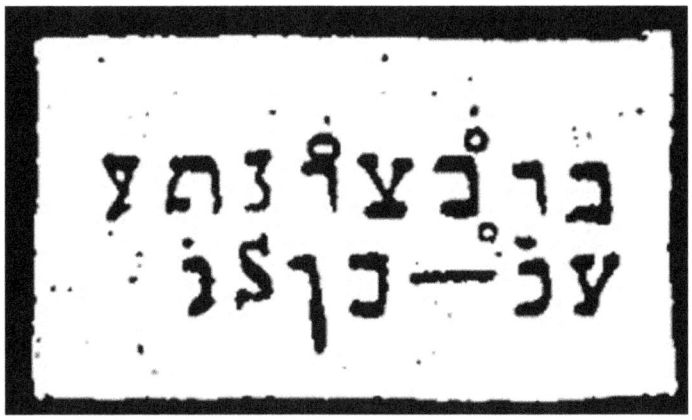

CHAPTER IX. MAGICAL LAWS OF MOSES

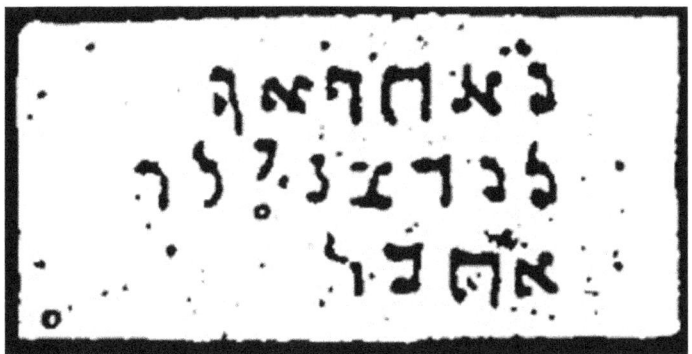

Conjuration

KUTA-AL, LEWUWAT--We are great! Our Hearts!

Prayer

Oh Lord, arise, that my enemies may be destroyed and that they may fly; that those who hate Thee may be scattered like smoke-

-drive them away. As wax melteth before the fire, so pass away all evil doers before God, for God has given thee the kingdom. Pour out Thy wrath over them. Thy wrath seize them. Thou shalt stand upon leopards and adders, and Thou shalt subdue the lion and dragon. With God only can we do great things. He will bring them under our feet.

CHAPTER X. HELMET OF MOSES AND AARON

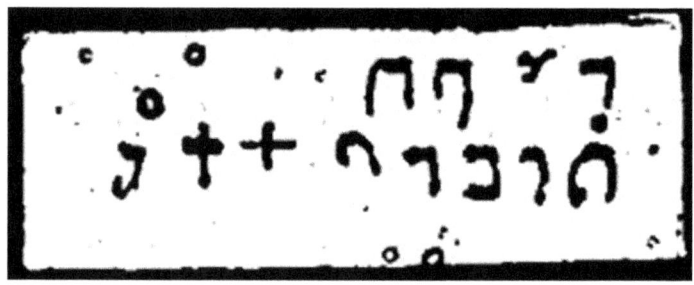

WOCHUTU, TUKAL, BESCHUFA, GUTAL--If I shall sin, I shall blow with the great horn.

Here the horn must be blown three times towards the four quarters of the earth. For the ram's horn, in the old covenant, is the symbol of omnipotence and of purification, or of beauty, truth and holiness.

CHAPTER XI. BREASTPLATE OF MOSES

Conjuration

SCHEDUSI, WEDUSE, TIWISI.--I have sinned, I shall sin.

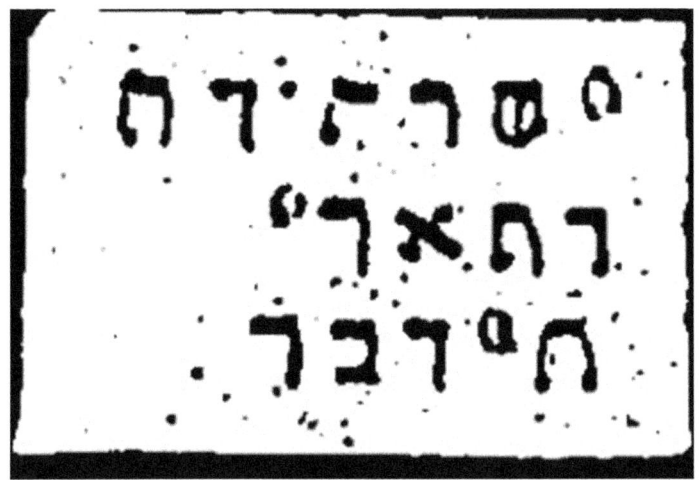

Prayer

Eternal God of our All! Our god! Hear our voice, spare and have mercy upon us. Accept our prayer in mercy and with pleasure. I have sinned. I have committed transgressions. I have sinned before Thee. I have done that which is displeasing unto Thee here in the earth. For the sake of Thy great name pardon me all the sins and iniquities and transgressions which I have committed against Thee from my youth. Perfect again all the holy names which I have blemished, Great Champion, terrible, highest God, eternal Lord, God Sabaoth.

CHAPTER XII. BREASTPLATE OF AARON

Conjuration

DEHUTU, EUWSALTU, BESCHOLAM--You have sinned. I shall sin in peace.

Prayer

The Lord, King of all Kings, holy and praised is He, the Father, God, Son of God, the Holy Spirit of God are three in one among these three. In the power of Thy might and Thy right, release those that are bound, receive the prayer of thy people, strengthen us, purify us, Oh terrible Hero, us who worship Thine name. Protect them as the apple of Thine eye, bless them, cleanse them, repay them always in mercy and justice. Mighty, Holy Lord, reward Thy congregation with Thy great goodness. Thou, the only and exalted God, appear unto thy people with Thy holy name; receive and remember our prayer; hearken unto our cries, Thou who knowest all secrets and who knowest our desire.

Here the horn must be blown as previously instructed.

CHAPTER XIII. THE CHALICE OF HOLINESS

Conjuration

Al, Al, Al--Arise, Thou eternal Angel!

This must be repeated three times in a loud voice, and the horn must also be blown three times, for he is an angel of the sanctuary.

Prayer

Thou that art, wast, and wilt be in the old and new covenant! Eternal, Jehovah, Jesus Christ, Messias, All Beautiful, All True, All Holy! All Loving and All Merciful in the old and in the new covenant. Thou hast said: Heaven and earth shall pass away, but my words shall not pass away. Thou hast said: I came not to destroy the old covenant, but to fulfill it. Thou hast said: He who sees me, sees the Father. Thou hast said: If ye have true faith, ye can perform the wonders which I have done, yea, ye will perform yet much greater wonders than I have done. Come also to me for the sake of my faith, come also unto me for the sake of Moses, Thy messenger of faith. Reveal also to me Thy mysterious name from Jehovah, as Thou once did to Thy fire prophet Moses in solitude. Come, and say unto me in love, through the heart of Moses and with the tongue of Aaron: SCAHEBUAL! I shall come!

FOR THE LEFT HAND

These signs were used at the time of burnt offerings in the holy temple.

FOR THE RIGHT HAND

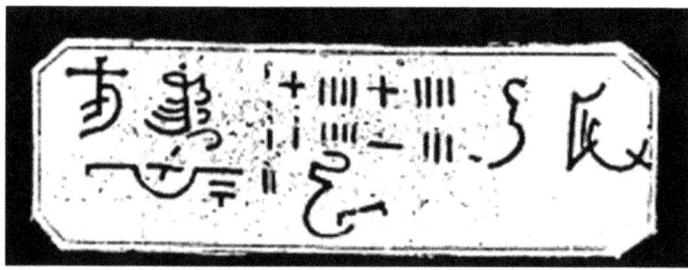

These are also symbolical of the plagues of Pharaoh in Egypt. SCHEMA ISRAEL ADONAI ELOHJEINU, ADONAI ECHAD.--Hear, O Israel, the Lord our God, the Lord is one.

BIBLIA ARCANA MAGICA ALEXANDER

TRADITION OF THE SIXTH BOOK OF MOSES

CHAPTER I. THE SPIRIT APPEARS IN A BURNING BUSH

CHAPTER II. MOSES CHANGES THE STAFF INTO A SERPENT

CHAPTER III. MOSES CHANGES WATER INTO BLOOD

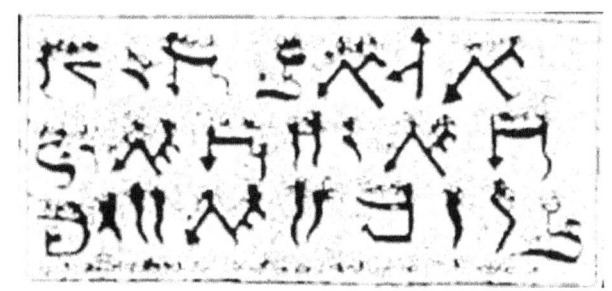

CHAPTER IV. THREE NEW SIGNS WITH FROGS, LICE AND SIMILAR VERMIN

CHAPTER V. THREE SIGNS OF CATTLE PESTILENCE BLACK SMALLPOX AND HAIL

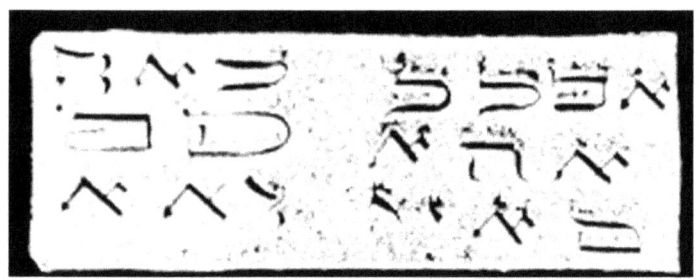

CHAPTER VI. THREE SIGNS WITH GRASSHOPPERS AND LOCUSTS

CHAPTER VI. GENERAL CITATION OF MOSES ON ALL SPIRITS

THE PENTAGON

TRADITION OF THE SEVENTH BOOK OF MOSES

CHAPTER I. THE SPIRIT APPEARS IN A PILLAR OF FIRE BY NIGHT

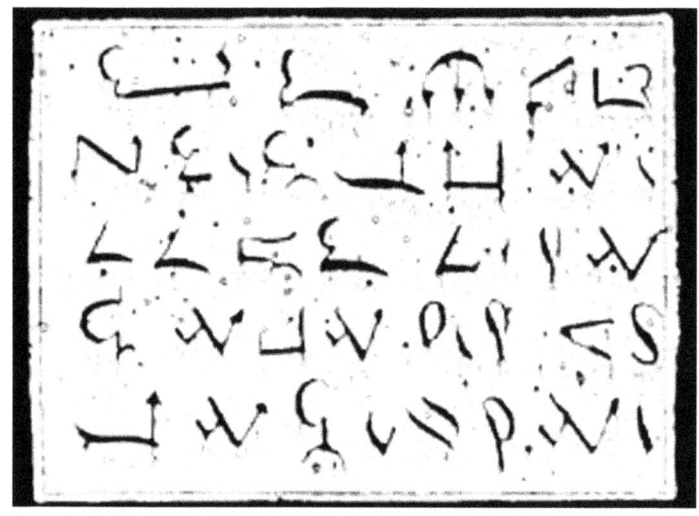

CHAPTER II. THE SPIRIT APPEARS IN A PILLAR OF CLOUD BY DAY

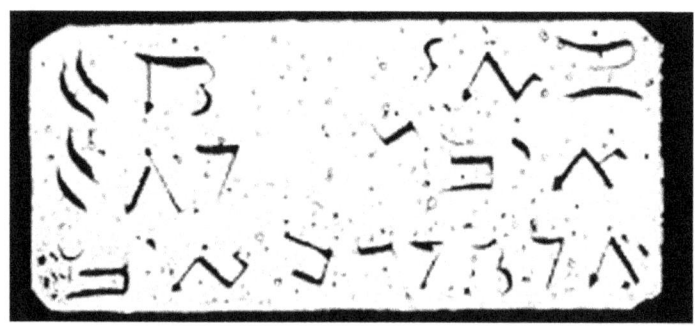

CHAPTER III. BALAAM'S SORCERY

CHAPTER IV. EGYPT

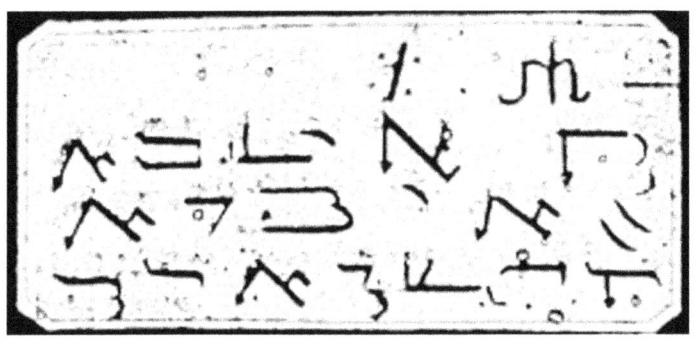

CHAPTER V. CONJURATION OF THE LAWS OF MOSES

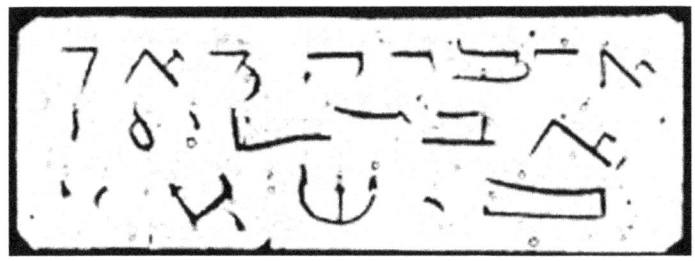

CHAPTER VI. GENERAL CITATION OF ALL SPIRITS

DISMISSAL OF MOSES

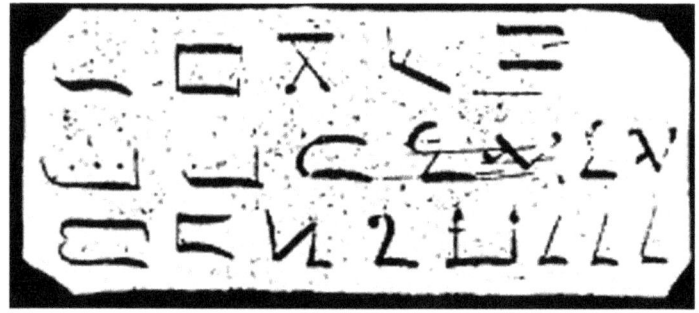

MAGICAL LAWS OF MOSES

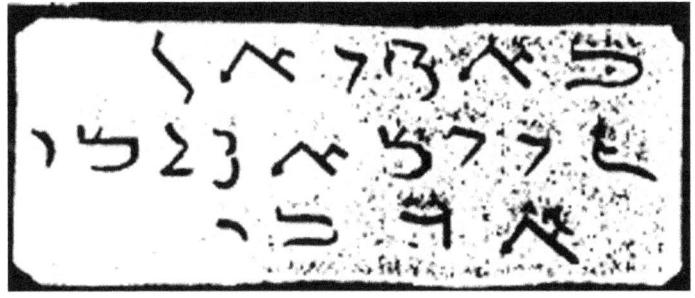

BREASTPLATE OF MOSES

HELMET OF MOSES AND AARON

BREASTPLATE OF AARON

FOR THE LEFT HAND

FOR THE RIGHT HAND

CONJURATION OF ELEAZAR

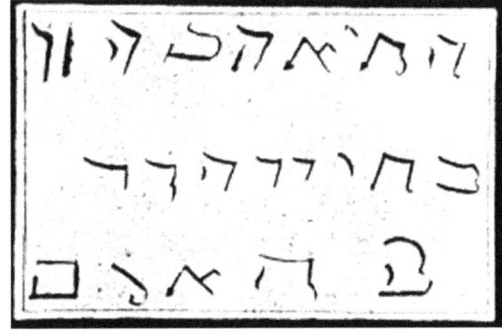

DISMISSAL OF ELEAZAR

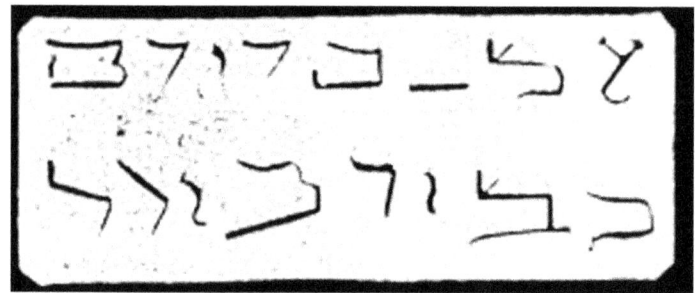

CITATION OF QUERMILLAM OR LEVIATHAN

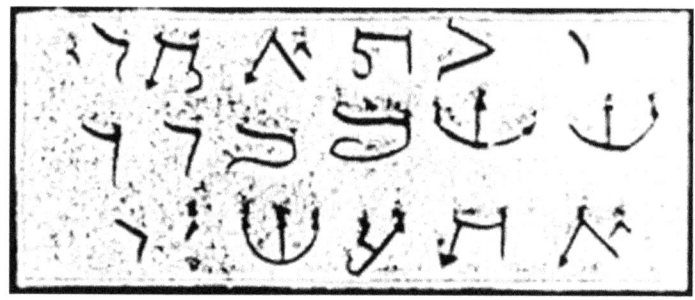

DISMISSAL OF QUERMILLAM OR LEVIATHAN

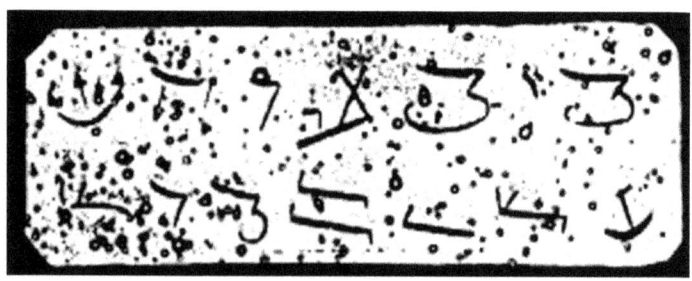

MAGICAL (SPIRIT COMMADO) BESIDE THE BLACK RAVEN

Romae ad Arcanum Pontificatus under Pope Alexander VI

Printed in 1501 AD

Instructions

If you want to compel spirits to appear visibly before you and render you obedience, observe the following instructions:

1. Keep God's commandments as much as possible.

2. Build and trust solely upon the might and power of God: believe firmly in his omnipotent help in your work, and the spirits will become your servants and will obey you.

3. Continue your citations and do not cease, even if the spirits do not appear at once. Be steadfast in your work and have faith, for the doubter will obtain nothing.

4. Take special note of the times for the invocation:

Monday night
from eleven until three.

Tuesday night
from ten until two

Wednesday night

from twelve until three

Thursday night
from twelve until two

Friday night
from ten until three

Saturday night
from ten until twelve

Sunday Sabbath
keep holy unto the Lord Sabaoth, Adonai, Tetragrammaton

5. The time must be the new moon, that is, the moon must be waxing.

6. Trace the circle {below} on parchment with the blood of Young white doves. The size of the circle is optional.

7. The circle must be consecrated before the ceremony, with the following words:

Ego (name of the conjuror), consecro et benedico istum circulum per Nomina Dei Attisimi in ec Scripta, ut sit mihi et omnibus Scutum et Protectio dei Fortissimi Elohim Invincibilie contra omnes malignos Spiritus, gerurmque Potestates. In Nomine Dei Patris Dei Filii Dei Spiritus Sancti. Amen.

Upon your entrance into this circle, speak as follows: Tetragrammaton, Theos, Ischiros, Athanatos, Messias, Imas, Kyrie Eleison. Amen.

After you have entered the circle, begin your operation with the following prayer from the Ninety-first psalm:

He that dwelleth in the secret place of the Most High shall abide under the shadow of the Almighty. I will say of the Lord, He is my refuge and my fortress, my God, in Him will I trust. Surely He shall deliver me from the snare of the fowler and from the noisome pestilence. He shall cover thee with His feathers and under his wings shalt thou trust. His truth shall be thy shield and thy buckler. Thou shalt not be afraid of the terror by night nor of the arrow that flieth by day. Because thou hast made the Lord, which is my refuge, even the Most High, thy habitation. There shall no evil befall thee, neither shall any plague come nigh thy dwelling. Because he has set his love upon me, therefore will I deliver him. I will set him on high because he has known my name. He will call upon me and I will answer him. I will be with him in trouble. I will deliver him and honor him. With long life will I satisfy him and show him My salvation. Even so help me and all them that seek thy holy God the Father God the Son God the Holy Ghost, Amen.

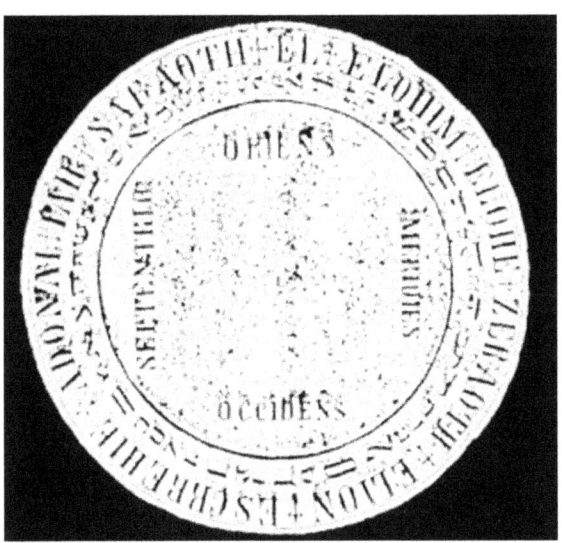

CIRCLE WRITTEN ON PARCHMENT

WITH THE

BLOOD OF WHITE YOUNG DOVES.

Citation of the Seven Great Princes

REMARKS

Following is some information regarding the appearances and provinces of the various spirits.

AZIEL
is a very prompt treasure spirit of the earth and of the sea. He appears in the form of a wild ox.

ARIEL
is a very serviceable spirit, and appears in the form of a ferocious dog. He commands the lost treasures of the land and sea.

MARBUEL
appears in the form of an old lion. He delivers the treasures of the water and of the land, and assists in obtaining all secret knowledge and honors.

MEPHISTOPHILIS
is ready to serve, and appears in the form of a youth. He is willing to serve in all skilled arts, and gives the spiritus Servos, otherwise called "familiars." He brings treasures from the earth and from the deep very quickly.

BARBUEL

is a master of all arts and all secret knowledge, a great master of all treasure. He is very accommodating, and appears with alacrity in the form of a wild hog.

AZIABEL
is a prince of the water and mountain spirits and their treasures. He is amiable and wears a large pearl crown.

ANITUEL
appears in the form of a serpent of paradise. He confers great wealth and honors according to wish.

Instructions

The seals or General Characters of the Seven Great Princes must be written upon virgin parchment with the blood of butterflies, at the time of the full moon. The Seven Great Princes have among them some of the legions of crown-spirits who were expelled from Heaven, according to tradition.

Mundus ater cum illis
Me pactum dicit habere
Sed me teque Deus
Te illo custodiat omnes.

CITATIONS AND SEALS

Citation of AZIEL

AZIELIS

Seal or Character for Coercion and Obedience.

Agla, Cadelo, Samba, Caclem, Awenhatoacoro, Aziel, Zorwotho, Yzeworth, Xoro, Quotwe, Theosy, Meweth, Xosoy, Yachyros, Gaba, Hagay, Staworo, Wyhaty, Ruoso Xuatho, Rum, Ruwoth, Zyros, Quaylos, Wewor, Vegath, Wysor, Wuzoy, Noses, * Aziel. *

Citation of Ariel

ARIELIS

Seal or Character for Coercion and Obedience.

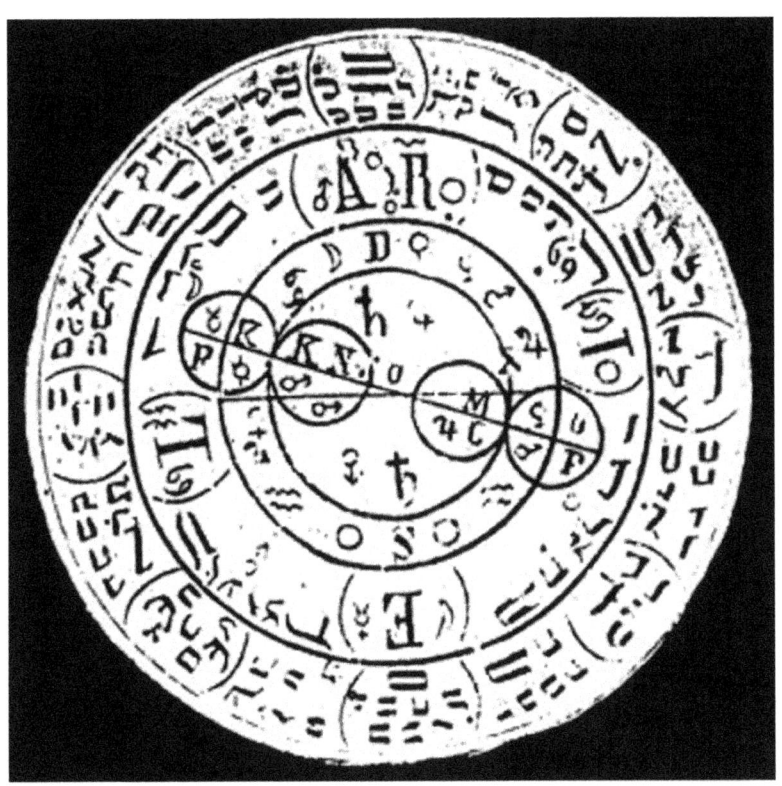

Yschiros, Theor Zebaoth, Wyzeth, Yzathos, Xyzo, Xywethororwoy, Xantho, Wiros, Rurawey, Ymowe, Noswathosway, Wuvnethowesy, Zebaoth, Yvmo, Zvswethonowe, Yschyrioskay, Ulathos, Wyzoy, Yrsawo, Xyzeth, Durobijthaos, Wuzowethus, Yzweoy, Zaday, Zywaye, Hagathorwos, Yachyros, Imas, Tetragrammaton, Ariel.

Citation of Marbuel

MARBUELIS

Seal or Character for Coercion and Obedience.

Adonay, Jehova, Zebaoth, Theos, Yzhathoroswe, Wehozymathos, Zosim, Yghoroy, Vegorym, Abaij, Wogos, Gijghijm, Zeowoij, Ykosowe, Wothym, Kijzwe, Uijwoth, Omegros, Hehgewe, Zebaoij, Wezator, Zibuo, Sijbetho, Ythos, Zeatijm, Wovoe, Sijwoijmwethij, Pharvoij, Zewor, Wegfos, Ruhen, Hvbathoroos, Stawows, Zijen, Zijwowij, Haros, Worse, Yzwet, Zebaoth, Agla, Marbuel.

Citation of Mephistophilis

MEPHISTOPHILIS

Seal or Character for Coercion and Obedience

Messias, Adonaij, Weforus, Xathor, Yxewe, Soraweijs, Yxaron, Wegharh, Zijhalor, Weghaij, Weosron, Xoxijwe, Zijwohwawetho, Ragthoswatho, Zebaoth, Adonaij, Zijwetho, Aglaij, Wijzathe, Zadaij, Zijebo, Xosthoy, Athlato, Zsewey, Zyxyset, Ysche, Sarsewu, Zyzyrn, Deworonhathbo, Xyxewe, Syzwe, Theos, Yschaos, Worsonbefgosy, Gefgowe, Hegor, Quaratho, Zywe, Messias, Abarabi, Mephistophilis.

Citation of Barbuel

BARBUELIS

Seal or Character for Coercion and Obedience.

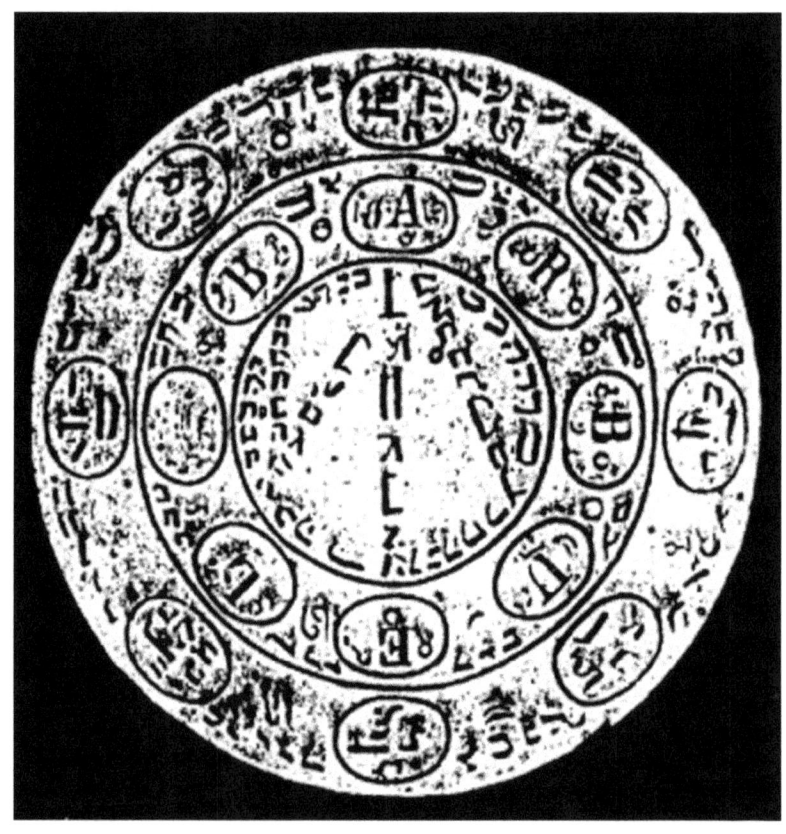

Yschiros, Imns, Zebaoth, Otheos, Kuwethosorym, Zylohym, Zaday, Yschowe, Quyos, Zenhatorowav, Yzwesor, Xywoy, Yzyryr, Zalijmo, Zabaoth, Adonaii, Messias, Aglabaij, Stoweos, Hijwetho, Ycoros, Zijwetho, Uwoim, Chamoweo, Zijzobeth, Sotho, Emnohalj, Zedije, Huwethos, Chorij, Yzquoos, Liraije, Weghoijm,

Xiixor, Waijos, Gofaljme, Toroswe, Yeijros, Emanuel, Imas, Barbuel.

Citation of Aziabel

AZIABELIS

Seal or Character for Coercion and Obedience.

Thoeos, Ygweto, Yzgowoij, Quiseo, Wijzope, Xorsoij, Nowetho, Yxose, Haguthou, Xoro, Theos, Magowo, Wijzosorwothe,

Xaroshaij, Zebaoth, Emanuel, Messias, Yzijwotho, Zadaij, Xexhatosijmeij, Buwatho, Ysewet, Xijrathor, Zijbos, Malhaton, Yzos, Uzewor, Raguil, Wewot, Yzewewe, Quorhijm, Zadob, Zibathor, Weget, Zijzawe, Ulijzor, Tetragrammaton, Aziabel.

Citation of Anituel

ANTQUELIS

Seal or Character for Coercion and Obedience.

Thoeos, Aba, Aaba, Aba, Agathoswaij, Yzoroij, Ywetho, Quardos, Quasoai, Uschjjros, Cijmoe, Qowathim, Geofoij, Zarobe, Weghatj, Ohegathorowaij, Mesows, Xalose, Waghthorsowe, Wephatho, Yzebo, Storilwethonaij, Quorathon, Sijbo, Mephor, Wijhose, Zaloros, Ruetho, Zebaathonaijwos, Zijweth, Ycarij, Ruwethonowe, Ruiathosowaij, Zebaoth, Messias, Anituel.

THE USE OF THE SEALS

If these great princes do not appear immediately on the foregoing Citations, or if they hesitate in their obedience, then cast frankincense and myrrh upon burning coals; when the smoke arises, place the spirit seal thereon, and pronounce the following mysterious words:

ALTISSIMA DIE VERBA

Spirituum Cactiva Mosis Aaron et Salomonis

Zijmuorsobet, Noijm, Zavaxo, Quehaij, Abawo, Noquetonaij, Oasaij, Wuram, Thefotoson, Zijoronoaifwetho, Mugelthor, Yzxe, Agiopuaij, Huzije, Surhatijm, Sowe, Oxursoij, Zijbo, Yzweth, Quaij, Salrthos, Quaij, Qeahaij, Qijrpu, Sardowe, Xoro, Wuggofhoswerhiz, Kaweko, Ykquos, Zehatho, Aba. Amen.

The Apparition

The conjured spirit will appear almost as soon as these word are said. As soon as he appears, address and compel him with the following words.

Binding Of Moses

Zebaoth, Abatho, Tetragrammaton, Adonaij, Abathoij, Zijhawe, Aglaij, Quohowe, Agla, Muijroshoweth, Phalowaij, Agla, Theos, Messias, Zijwethororijm, Feghowo, Aba, Mowewo, Choe, Adonaij, Cewoe, Christohatos, Tetragrammaton.

Instructions

Since the spirits will now appear quickly, express your desires to them clearly, honestly and without fear for nothing can harm you. Rather they must serve you obediently and give your all you require of them. However, remember not to compromise with any spirits in any way, do not yield to them in any way, and be firm in your demeanor. For these words of might and power that you have used in the conjuration are sufficient to compel the spirits to obey you and to do so without harm or deception.

MIHI FAUSTO EXPERTO

VALEDICTO OR DISMISSAL OF THE SPIRITS

Since the spirits have now served you according to your wishes, dismiss them and discharge them with the following words:

Zebaoth, Theos, Yschyres, Messias, Imas, Weghaymnko, Quoheos, Roveym, Christoze, Abay, Xewefaraym, Agla.

And now depart in the name of God. Praise, love and thank God to the end.

THE RABELLINI TABLE

Monarchy of the Good and Familiar Spirits

The following angelic spirits can be cited for all human ministrations: Seraphim Uriel, Cherubim Raphael, Thronus Oriphiel, Dominatio Zachariel, Potestas Gabriel, Virtus Barbiel, Principatus Requel, Archangelus Anael, Angelus Phaleg.

These are the Princes of the nine Choir of Angels. They have among them many spirits 1,000 times 1,000 without end. Sanctus, Sanctus, Sanctus.

These angelic spirits appear very willingly to human beings to help and serve them in all things.

Other Good Spirits

Chymchy, Asbeor, Yzazel, Xomoy, Asmoy, Diema, Bethor, Arfose, Zenay, Corowe, Orowor, Xonor, Quilheth, Quato, Wewor, Gefowe, Gorhon, Woreth, Hagyr, Welor.

Archarontica or Evil Spirits

Even though evil, the following spirits are still familiar or ministering spirits, and are ready to serve.

Thebot, Wethor, Quorthonn, Ywote, Yrson, Xysorym, Zuwoy, Puchon, Tulef, Legioh, Xexor, Woryon.

Instructions

Concerning white magic, take notice that all good spirits must be cited when the moon is full, the Princes of the nine Choir of Angels, as well as the other good spirits.

Concerning black magic, take notice that the Seven Princes of Evil must be cited during new moon. Other evil spirits are cited most readily in the dark of the moon, or at the time of an eclipse of the sun or the moon. The circle already {above}, as coercive of hell, is to be used for all spirits, good or evil.

General Citation of Moses, Aaron and Solomon for All Spirits

Aba, Alpha, Omega, Hewozywetony, Xewerator, Menhatoy, Queo, Zuwezet, Rumoy, Ruwetze, Quano, Duzy, Zenthono-Rohmatru, Xono, Zonozebethoos, Zebaoth, Aglay, Tetragrammaton, Adonay, Theos, Ysehyroroseth, Zumquvos, Nywe, Athanatos, Thoy, Quyhet, Homor, Wethoum, Ywae, Ysgeboth, Oray, Zywo, Ysgewot, Zururogos, Zuy, Zywethorosto, Rurom, Xuwye, Xunewe, Keoso, Wecato, Zyweso, Tetragrammaton.

Now pronounce the name of the good or evil
 spirit distinctly that you wish to conjure. He will appear very suddenly. You then may address him.

Coercion or Binding Of Spirits

Theohatatos, Quyseym, Gefgowe, Phagayr, Messias. Amen.

Valedictio or Dismissal of Spirits

Theos, Zebaoth, Adonay, Ischiros, Zaday, Messias, Salomos, Yweth, Thors, Yzheto, Thyym, Quowe, Xehatoym, Phoe, Tetragrammaton.

Now pronounce the name of the spirit and let him depart in peace. Deus Principium et Finis.

www.ingramcontent.com/pod-product-compliance
Lightning Source LLC
Chambersburg PA
CBHW051551010526
44118CB00022B/2656